WINDOWS
WITH *Style*

**CREATIVE
PUBLISHING
international**

MINNETONKA, MINNESOTA

www.howtobookstore.com

CONTENTS

Library of Congress
Cataloging-in-Publication Data

Windows with style : do-it-yourself window
treatments.
     p. cm.
   Includes index.
   ISBN 0-86573-349-x (hardcover)
   1. Drapery. 2. Blinds. 3. Window shades.
4. Drapery in interior decoration.
   I. Creative Publishing international. Inc.
TT390.W553 1997
746.9'4 -- dc21   97-15643

CREATIVE
PUBLISHING
international

President/CEO: Michael Eleftheriou

Created by: The Editors of
Creative Publishing international, Inc.
Printed on American paper by:
R. R. Donnelley & Sons Co.
10 9

WINDOW TREATMENT STYLES

*With careful style selection,
window treatments can be
both functional and beautiful.*

Window treatments have a great impact on the decorating scheme of a room. Depending on the style of the treatment and the fabric selected, a window can become a dramatic focal point in the room. Or it can blend with the wall treatment, creating a subtle background and allowing the furniture to take center stage. Style choices vary from simple, informal treatments, such as fabric roller shades or scarf swags, to boldly formal layered curtains and elaborate top treatments.

Along with the decorative aspects of the window treatment, there are a few functional needs to consider. Bedroom windows, for instance, may require a high degree of light control, while window treatments in the dining room may be selected because they allow light to fill the room. Treatments that offer privacy may be necessary on windows that face a busy street, while windows that open onto a beautiful, secluded landscape may be dressed with minimal treatments that merely enhance the view.

Whether you are starting with bare windows or adding to existing treatments, such as pleated shades or blinds, you can select a window treatment that reflects your personal taste. Careful selection of style, fabric, and hardware helps ensure the success of your window treatment project.

SELECTING A STYLE

Aside from the decorative and functional aspects of the window treatment, also consider the structural details of the window itself, including the way it operates. The treatment must be designed to allow easy access if the window will be opened and closed regularly. You may want to accent a decorative window frame or select a style that will cover inferior woodwork around the window. Also take note of any structural details near the window that may affect the size or style of the treatment, such as built-in cabinets, electrical switches, doors, heat registers, or other windows.

Often the window treatment you select will be a combination of two or more styles. One style, selected for its functional characteristics, may be combined with another decorative style to satisfy all the needs of the treatment. For consistency, combine styles that reflect the same decorating theme. Some choices, such as fabric roller shades and scarf swags, are versatile and can be combined successfully with many other styles.

Snapshots of windows serve as visual aides when selecting window treatments. Take a photograph of the window, closing any existing undertreatments that will remain; catch the ceiling line and floor in the photograph. Cover the photograph with a sheet of clear plastic or acetate, and, using a dry-erase marker, sketch the desired treatment.

Rod-pocket curtains with welted heading (page 105) are tied back with shaped tiebacks (page 114). Scarf swag valance (page 142) is mounted over the top of the curtains, allowing the heading to show.

Ruffled rod-pocket swag (page 133) is an elegant complement to these sheer rod-pocket curtains (page 82).

Soft cornice with overlapping panels (page 184) softens the contemporary look of vertical blinds.

Stagecoach valance (page 160) is mounted inside the window frame.

Straw hats hung from a peg rail (page 218) make an interesting alternative-style valance.

Unlined rod-pocket curtains have a flounce heading (page 104) and shaped tiebacks (page 114). African violets add a touch of color to the treatment (page 199).

Hourglass curtains (page 95) are the perfect treatment for French doors.

(Continued)

SELECTING A STYLE
(CONTINUED)

Slatted Roman shades (page 46) have a sleek, contemporary look, which is also carried out by the buttoned valance (page 166).

Split hourglass curtains (page 100) frame a frosted design (page 205) on a door window.

Hanging plant shelf (page 194) is a functional alternative window treatment.

Rod-pocket curtains with double ruffles (page 90) are layered over a fabric roller shade (page 28). Ruffled tiebacks (page 115) complete the look.

Scarf swags with poufs (page 142) are an elegant top treatment over pleated shades.

Shoji-style screen (page 208) is a simplified version of the traditional Japanese window treatment.

Hobbled Roman shade (page 41), mounted outside the window frame, is an understated treatment for a small window.

Lined rod-pocket curtains (page 83) mounted on a PVC pole with elbows (page 14) are held back gracefully with decorative holdbacks (page 10).

Hourglass curtains (page 95) and split hourglass curtains (page 100) are combined to make a unique treatment for this triple window.

Triple rod-pocket swag (page 136) with tassel fringe trim is a soft yet dramatic top treatment over sheer curtains.

HARDWARE NEEDS

Whether your window treatment is stationary or traversing, the hardware you select can be decorative as well as functional. For ornate window treatments, traditional wood or metal poles with detailed finials are available, as well as decorative tieback holders. And sleek, contemporary hardware is available for a more understated look. Some treatment styles cover the rod entirely, calling for less expensive, nondecorative utility hardware.

Select and install the hardware you want before measuring for a window treatment. The cut length of fabric panels for curtains, draperies, and valances depends on the style and placement of the hardware.

DECORATIVE HARDWARE

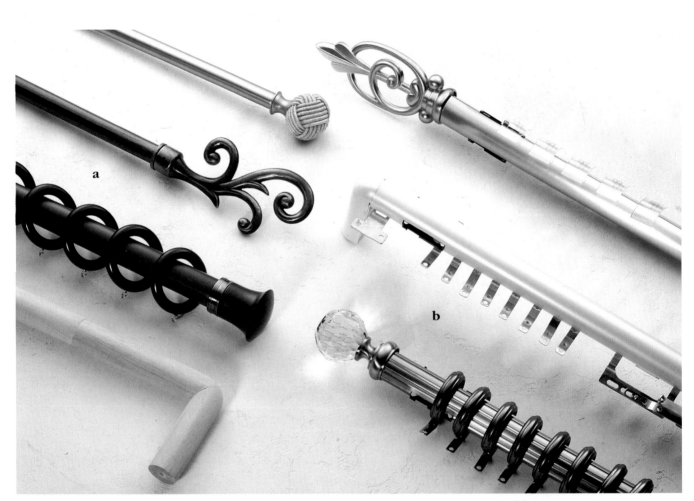

Metal rods and wood poles (a) in various finishes and diameters are used with rings for hand-drawn traversing or stationary treatments when part or all of the rod or pole is always exposed. Without the rings, the rods and poles are suitable for swags or for stationary rod-pocket or tab styles. Stylish finials accompany the metal rods; wood poles may have finials or elbows. Unfinished wood poles can be painted, stained, or covered with fabric to fit perfectly into your decor.

Decorative traverse rods (b) have a built-in mechanism of carriers and cording for opening and closing the treatment. Most often used for pleated draperies, the rods can have plain carriers or ring carriers. Tab carriers are also available, for hanging traversing tab curtains.

UTILITY HARDWARE

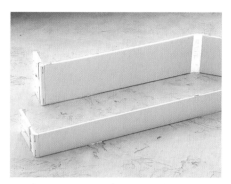

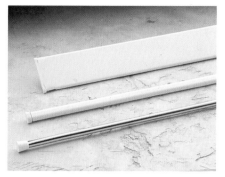

Narrow curtain rods are used for rod-pocket window treatments. They are available in various projections in single and double rod styles.

Wide curtain rods are available in 2½" (6.5 cm) and 4½" (11.5 cm) widths. They add depth and interest to rod-pocket window treatments. Corner connectors make these rods suitable for bay and corner windows, also.

Tension rods, used inside window frames for rod-pocket curtains and valances, are held in place by the pressure of a spring inside the rod. Because mounting brackets are not used, the woodwork is not damaged by screws.

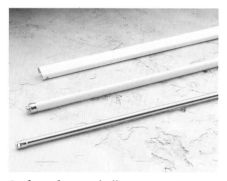

Sash rods use shallow mounting brackets so the window treatment hangs close to the glass. Available flat or round, they are commonly used for stretched curtains on doors.

Conventional traverse rods, designed for pleated draperies, are available in white, ivory, and wood tones. Drapery hooks are inserted so the pleats conceal the rod when the treatment is closed. Valances or cornices are used over the top of the draperies to completely conceal the rod.

Flexible traverse rods are used for pleated draperies on bow windows.

HARDWARE ACCESSORIES

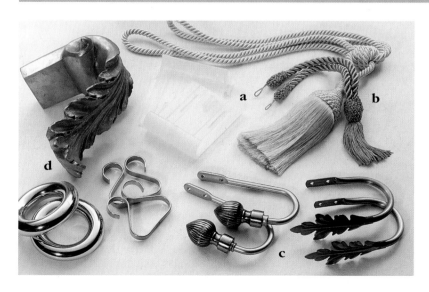

Concealed tieback holders (a) fit behind the last fold of pleated or rod-pocket draperies to prevent the tieback from crushing the draperies. The projection is adjustable.

Cord-and-tassel tiebacks (b) are used with concealed or decorative holders to hold draperies in place.

Holdbacks (c), as the name implies, are decorative accessories that hold back a stationary curtain or drapery without the use of tiebacks.

Swag holders (d), in a wide range of styles, support the draped fabric in swag window treatments. Some styles are meant to be concealed, while others are quite obviously decorative.

INSTALLING HARDWARE

Window treatment hardware is packaged complete with mounting brackets, screws or nails, and installation instructions. Use screws alone if installing through drywall or plaster directly into wall studs. When brackets are positioned between wall studs, support the screws for lightweight treatments with plastic anchors in the correct size for the screws. If the brackets must support a heavy window treatment, use plastic toggle anchors in the correct size for the wallboard depth, or use molly bolts. If nails are supplied with the hardware you purchased, use them only for lightweight treatments installed directly to the window frame. Otherwise, substitute screws or molly bolts that fit through the holes in the brackets.

HOW TO INSTALL HARDWARE USING PLASTIC ANCHORS

1 Mark the screw locations on the wall. Drill holes for the plastic anchors, using a drill bit slightly smaller than the diameter of the plastic anchor. Tap the plastic anchors into the drilled holes, using a hammer.

2 Insert the screw through the hole in the hardware and into installed plastic anchor. Tighten the screw securely; the anchor expands in drywall, preventing it from pulling out of the wall.

HOW TO INSTALL HARDWARE USING PLASTIC TOGGLE ANCHORS

1 Mark screw locations on wall. Drill holes for plastic toggle anchors, using drill bit slightly smaller than diameter of toggle anchor shank.

2 Squeeze the wings of the toggle anchor flat, and push toggle anchor into hole; tap in with hammer until it is flush with wall.

3 Insert the screw through hole in hardware and into installed anchor; tighten screw. Wings spread out and flatten against back side of drywall.

HOW TO INSTALL HARDWARE USING MOLLY BOLTS

1 Mark screw locations on wall. Drill holes for molly bolts, using drill bit slightly smaller than diameter of the molly bolt.

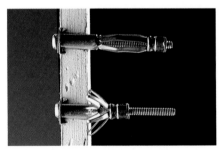

2 Tap the molly bolt into the drilled hole, using hammer; tighten screw. Molly bolt expands and flattens against back side of drywall.

3 Remove screw from molly bolt; insert the screw through hole in hardware and into installed molly bolt. Screw hardware securely in place.

INSTALLING PVC POLES

Pvc pipe can be used as a lightweight and inexpensive alternative to wood or metal decorator poles. PVC pipe is available in a variety of sizes, with inside diameters ranging from 1" to 4" (2.5 to 10 cm). PVC elbows, available in each size, can be used to make a pole with returns. Or, if desired, decorator finials can be attached to the ends of the PVC pole.

MATERIALS

FOR POLES WITH FINIALS

- PVC pipe in desired diameter; select size of pipe to fit end of finial.
- Two decorator finials.
- Keyhole support brackets, for ends and center supports; ½" (1.3 cm) hex-head screws.
- 1½" (3.8 cm) hex-head screws, for installing brackets into wall studs; or molly bolts or toggle anchors, for installing into drywall or plaster.
- Scrap of wood.
- Sandpaper; hacksaw; drill and drill bits.

FOR POLES WITH ELBOW RETURNS

- PVC pipe in desired diameter.
- Two PVC elbows, preferably without collars, in size to match pipe.
- Keyhole support brackets, for center supports; ½" (1.3 cm) hex-head screws.
- Two 2" (5 cm) angle irons, for mounting at returns.
- 1½" (3.8 cm) flat-head screws, for installing angle irons into wall studs; or molly bolts or toggle anchors, for installing into drywall or plaster.
- Two 10 × 1" (2.5 cm) round-head bolts.

HOW TO MAKE & INSTALL A PVC POLE WITH FINIALS

1 Cut PVC pipe to the desired length, using a hacksaw; sand the ends. Cut a scrap of wood to wedge snugly into each end of the pipe. Drill a hole in center of each wood scrap, using a drill bit slightly smaller than the finial screw. Insert the wood scraps into ends of the pole.

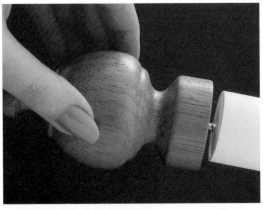

2 Attach finial to wood scrap. Repeat for the opposite end of the pole.

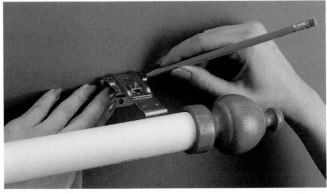

3 Hold the pole to the wall at desired location; mark for placement of keyhole support brackets on wall, at least ½" (1.3 cm) from finials. If additional support bracket is needed, mark for placement near center. Install brackets, using 1½" (3.8 cm) hex-head screws, into wall studs; if brackets are not positioned at the wall studs, use molly bolts or toggle anchors (page 12).

4 Hold pole up to the brackets; mark placement for ½" (1.3 cm) screws on back of the pole. Predrill holes for screws; insert screws into the holes, leaving heads of screws standing slightly away from back of the pole. Mount pole, inserting the screw heads into the keyholes.

HOW TO MAKE & INSTALL A PVC POLE WITH ELBOW RETURNS

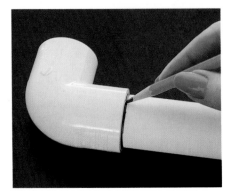

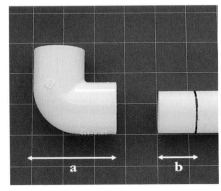

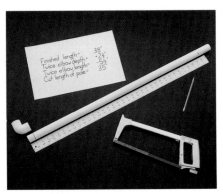

1 Slide elbow onto the pipe as far as possible; mark the depth of elbow on the pipe.

2 Remove elbow; measure the elbow length **(a)** from the outer edge of one side to the opening on the opposite side. Then measure the elbow depth **(b)** from end of pipe to the mark.

3 Cut the PVC pipe, using hacksaw, with length equal to the desired finished length of the pole plus twice the elbow depth minus twice the elbow length. Sand the cut ends.

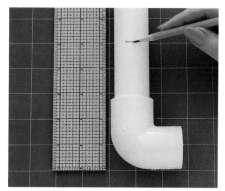 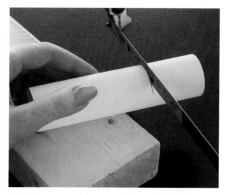 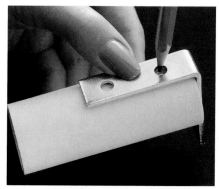

4 Slide the elbow onto a small remaining piece of PVC pipe as far as possible. Measure from the outer edge of elbow to the desired return depth on pipe; mark.

5 Remove the pipe from the elbow. Cut the pipe with a hacksaw; cut a second piece the same length for the opposite return. Sand the cut ends.

6 Lay angle iron over end of return pipe; mark pipe with location of hole closest to the back of angle iron. Drill hole through marked side of the pipe, using a ¼" drill bit. Repeat for the second return pipe.

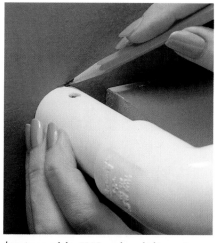  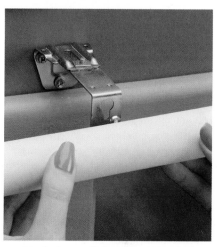

7 Assemble PVC pole, sliding pipe pieces into the elbows as far as possible, with holes in return pieces centered on top. Hold pole to wall in the desired location; mark wall at top center of return piece.

8 Mount angle irons on wall, with tops of angle irons centered at the marks, using 1½" (3.8 cm) flat-head screws into wall studs; if angle irons are not positioned at wall studs, use molly bolts or toggle anchors (page 12). Mount pole over angle irons, aligning holes in pipe to holes in angle irons; insert 10 × 1" (2.5 cm) round-head bolts through holes to secure.

9 Mark the wall for center keyhole support bracket, if needed; mark placement for screw on back of pole. Remove pole; install bracket on wall, and insert screw into back of pole, as in step 4, opposite. Remount pole.

HOW TO HANG ROD-POCKET CURTAINS ON A PVC POLE

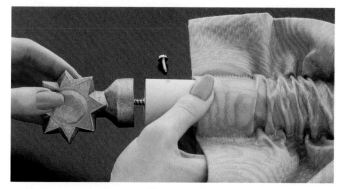 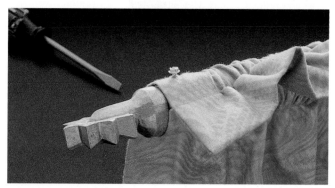

1 Remove pole from wall; remove screws, if any, from the back of pole. Remove elbows or finials. Insert the pole into rod pocket of the curtain; reattach finials or elbows. Distribute fullness evenly.

2 Locate screw holes, if any, and insert screws through curtain fabric. Remount the pole on the brackets or angle irons.

INSTALLING MOUNTING BOARDS

Many window treatments are mounted on boards rather than on drapery hardware. The mounting board is usually covered with fabric to match the window treatment or with drapery lining, and the window treatment is then stapled to the board. The mounting board can be installed as an outside mount, securing it directly to the window frame or to the wall above and outside the window frame. Or the board may be installed as an inside mount by securing it inside the window frame.

The size of the mounting board varies, depending on whether the board-mounted window treatment is an inside or outside mount and whether it is being used alone or with an undertreatment. When using stock, or nominal, lumber, keep in mind that the actual measurement differs from the nominal measurement. A 1 × 2 board measures ¾" × 1½" (2 × 3.8 cm), a 1 × 4 measures ¾" × 3½" (2 × 9 cm), a 1 × 6 measures ¾" × 5½" (2 × 14 cm), and a 1 × 8 measures ¾" × 7¼" (2 × 18.7 cm).

For an inside-mounted window treatment, the depth of the window frame must be at least 1½" (3.8 cm), to accommodate a 1 × 2 mounting board. Cut the mounting board ½" (1.3 cm) shorter than the inside measurement across the window frame, to ensure that the board will fit inside the frame when it is covered with fabric.

The projection necessary for outside-mounted top treatments depends on the projection of any existing undertreatments. If the undertreatment is stationary, allow at least 2" (5 cm) of clearance between it and the top treatment; if the undertreatment traverses, allow at least 3" (7.5 cm) clearance. If there is no undertreatment or if the undertreatment is mounted inside the window frame, use a 1 × 4 board for the top treatment. Cut the mounting board at least 2" (5 cm) wider than the outside measurement across the window frame. Install the board using angle irons that measure more than one-half the projection of the board.

For an outside-mounted Roman shade, use a 1 × 2 board. Screw the board flat to the wall for a ¾" (2 cm) projection; this allows the shade to rest close to the window frame. For a 1½" (3.8 cm) projection, install the board on edge, using angle irons.

HOW TO COVER THE MOUNTING BOARD

CUTTING DIRECTIONS

Cut the fabric to cover the mounting board, with the width of the fabric equal to the distance around the mounting board plus 1" (2.5 cm) and the length of the fabric equal to the length of the mounting board plus 3" (7.5 cm).

1 Center board on the wrong side of the fabric. Staple one long edge of fabric to board, placing staples about 8" (20.5 cm) apart; do not staple within 6" (15 cm) of ends. Wrap the fabric around board. Fold under ⅜" (1 cm) on long edge; staple to board, placing staples about 6" (15 cm) apart.

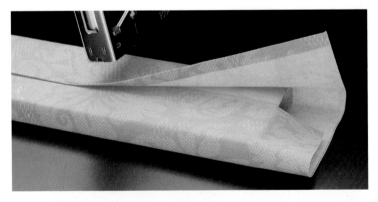

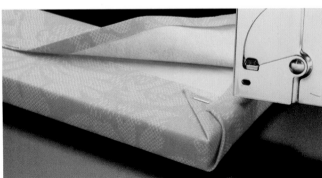

2 Miter fabric at corners on side of board with unfolded fabric edge; finger-press. Staple miters in place near raw edge.

3 Miter fabric at corners on side of board with folded fabric edge; finger-press. Fold under excess fabric at ends; staple near fold.

HOW TO INSTALL AN INSIDE-MOUNTED BOARD

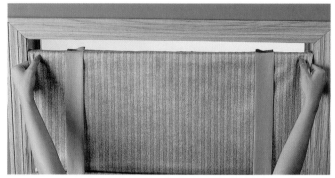

1 Cover mounting board (opposite). Attach the window treatment to the mounting board. Hold board in place against upper window frame, with wide side of board up; align front of treatment with front edge of frame.

2 Predrill screw holes through the board and up into the window frame, using ⅛" drill bit; drill holes within 1" (2.5 cm) of each end of the board and in center for wide window treatments. Adjust placement of holes to avoid screw eyes, if any. Secure the board, using 8 × 1½" (3.8 cm) round-head screws.

HOW TO INSTALL AN OUTSIDE-MOUNTED BOARD

1 Cover mounting board (opposite). Attach window treatment to board. Mark screw holes for angle irons on bottom of board, positioning angle irons within 1" (2.5 cm) of each end of board and at 45" (115 cm) intervals or less; adjust the placement to avoid screw eyes, if any.

2 Predrill screw holes into board; size of drill bit depends on screw size required for angle iron. Screw angle irons to board.

3 Hold board at desired placement, making sure it is level; mark the screw holes on wall or window frame. Remove angle irons from board.

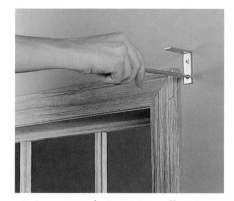

4 Secure angle irons to wall, using 1½" (3.8 cm) flat-head screws, into wall studs; if angle irons are not positioned at wall studs, use molly bolts or toggle anchors instead of flat-head screws.

5 Reposition window treatment on angle irons, aligning screw holes; fasten screws.

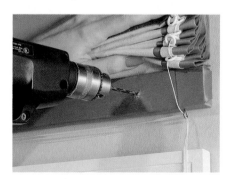

Roman shade mounted with ¾" (2 cm) projection. Install board flat to wall at desired location above window, predrilling holes through board into wall. Secure with 8 × 2½" (6.5 cm) flat-head screws into wall studs, if possible; or use molly bolts or toggle anchors if not screwing into wall studs.

MEASURING

Sketch the window treatment to scale on graph paper, to help you determine the most pleasing proportion for the treatment as well as the correct placement of any necessary hardware. After installing the hardware, take all necessary measurements of the window, using a steel tape measure for accuracy, and record the measurements on the sketch.

Window treatments may be mounted inside or outside the window frame, depending on the style of the treatment and the depth of the frame. For an inside mount, the frame must be deep enough to allow the treatment to be mounted flush with the front of the frame and without interfering with the operation of the window. For an outside mount, the hardware may be mounted on the window frame or on the wall outside the frame, high enough to allow any center support brackets to clear the frame.

For each project, you will need to determine the finished length and width of the treatment. The finished length is measured from the top of the mounting board, rod, or heading to where you want the lower edge of the window treatment. The finished width is determined by measuring the length of the rod or mounting board; for treatments with returns, add twice the projection of the rod or mounting board.

Specific instructions for determining the cut lengths and widths of the fabric are given for each project in this book. Yardage requirements can be determined by multiplying the cut length by the number of fabric widths needed to obtain the cut width. When estimating the yardage for patterned fabric, add the length of one pattern repeat for each fabric width needed, to allow for matching the patterns.

TIPS FOR MEASURING

Plan the proportion of the layers in a window treatment so the length of the top treatment is about one-fifth the length of the undertreatment. The top treatment may be installed higher than the window, to add visual height to the overall treatment. In some cases, it may be desirable to start the top treatment at the ceiling, provided the top of the window frame is not visible at the lower edge of the top treatment.

Plan for the shortest point of a top treatment to fall at least 4" to 6" (10 to 15 cm) below the top of the window glass. This prevents you from seeing the window frame as you look upward at the top treatment.

Allow ½" (1.3 cm) clearance between the lower edge of the curtain panels and the floor when measuring for floor-length curtains. Allow 1" (2.5 cm) clearance for loosely woven fabrics, because the curtains may stretch slightly after they are hung.

Allow 4" to 6" (10 to 15 cm) clearance above baseboard heaters, for safety.

Plan window treatments to avoid covering heat registers or cold-air returns, for good air circulation.

Measure for all curtains in the room to the same height from the floor, for a uniform look. Use the highest window in the room as the standard for measuring the other windows.

Finished width of window treatment or length of rod or mounting board plus returns

Outside frame

Inside frame

Finished length of window treatment

Finished length of window to sill

Finished length of window to apron

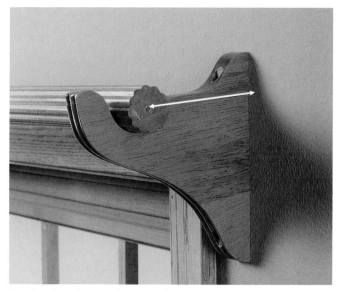

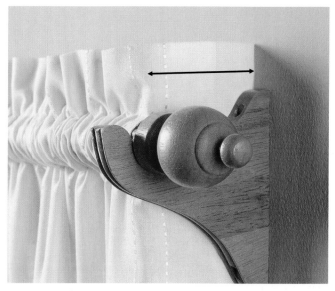

Projection is the distance the rod or mounting board stands out from the wall. When a wood pole is used, the projection is the distance from the wall to the center of the pole.

Return is the portion of the curtain or top treatment extending from the end of the rod or mounting board to the wall, enclosing the brackets and blocking the side light and view.

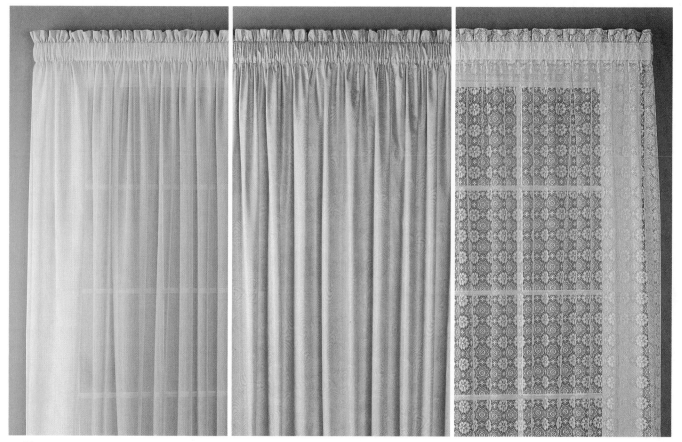

Fullness describes the finished width of the curtain panels in proportion to the length of the rod. For example, two times fullness means that the width of the curtain measures two times the length of the rod. For sheer and lightweight fabrics, use two-and-one-half to three times fullness (left). For mediumweight to heavyweight fabrics, use two to two-and-one-half times fullness (center). For lace curtains, one-and-one-half to two times fullness is often used, allowing the pattern in the lace to be more apparent (right).

BASIC SEWING TECHNIQUES

When sewing window treatments, a few basic guidelines help ensure good results. The techniques vary somewhat, depending on the type of fabric you are sewing. For any project, it is important to preshrink fabric and lining, using a steam iron, before they are cut.

Many decorator fabrics are tightly woven and may be cut perpendicular to the selvage, using a carpenter's square as a guide for marking the cutting line. However, because lightweight and loosely woven fabrics, such as sheers and casements, tend to slide easily as you cut, it is easier and more accurate to pull a thread along the crosswise grain and cut along the pulled thread.

Patterned decorator fabrics are designed to be matched at the seams (opposite). For soft cornices, stagecoach valances, and other window treatments with wide, flat expanses of fabric, it is desirable to eliminate seams by railroading the fabric whenever possible (opposite).

Many window treatments look better and are more durable if they are lined. Lining adds body to the treatment as well as protection from sunlight. Some linings are treated to be water-resistant, while others provide a higher degree of energy efficiency or light control. Blackout lining (opposite) not only blocks the sunlight, but also helps to conceal seams and hems.

TYPES OF SEAMS

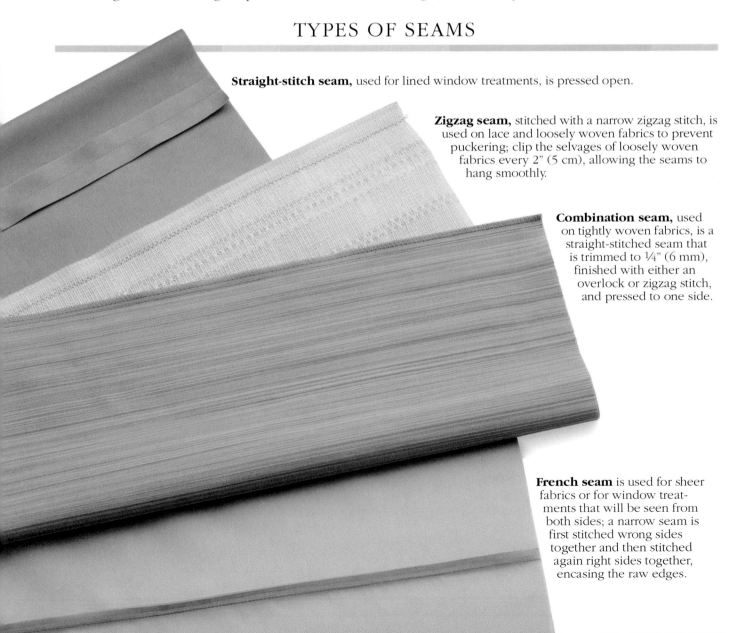

Straight-stitch seam, used for lined window treatments, is pressed open.

Zigzag seam, stitched with a narrow zigzag stitch, is used on lace and loosely woven fabrics to prevent puckering; clip the selvages of loosely woven fabrics every 2" (5 cm), allowing the seams to hang smoothly.

Combination seam, used on tightly woven fabrics, is a straight-stitched seam that is trimmed to ¼" (6 mm), finished with either an overlock or zigzag stitch, and pressed to one side.

French seam is used for sheer fabrics or for window treatments that will be seen from both sides; a narrow seam is first stitched wrong sides together and then stitched again right sides together, encasing the raw edges.

MATCHING PATTERNED FABRICS

1 Position fabric widths right sides together, matching selvages. Fold back upper selvage until the pattern matches; press foldline.

2 Unfold selvage, and pin the fabric widths together on foldline. Check the match from right side.

3 Repin the fabric so the pins are perpendicular to foldline; stitch on the foldline, using straight stitch.

CONSTRUCTION TIPS

Railroad fabric by running the lengthwise grain horizontally on window treatments with wide, flat expanses, as shown in the soft cornice at left. If fabric is not railroaded, as shown in the example at right, it is necessary to seam the fabric. Railroading is appropriate for fabrics with solid colors or nondirectional patterns.

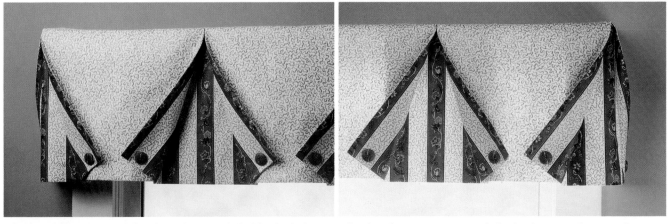

Blackout lining, used for the valance at left, blocks light completely. This prevents unsightly shadowing of seams, hems, or designs from the back of the treatment onto the front, as shown in the example at right.

Window
Shades

FABRIC ROLLER SHADES

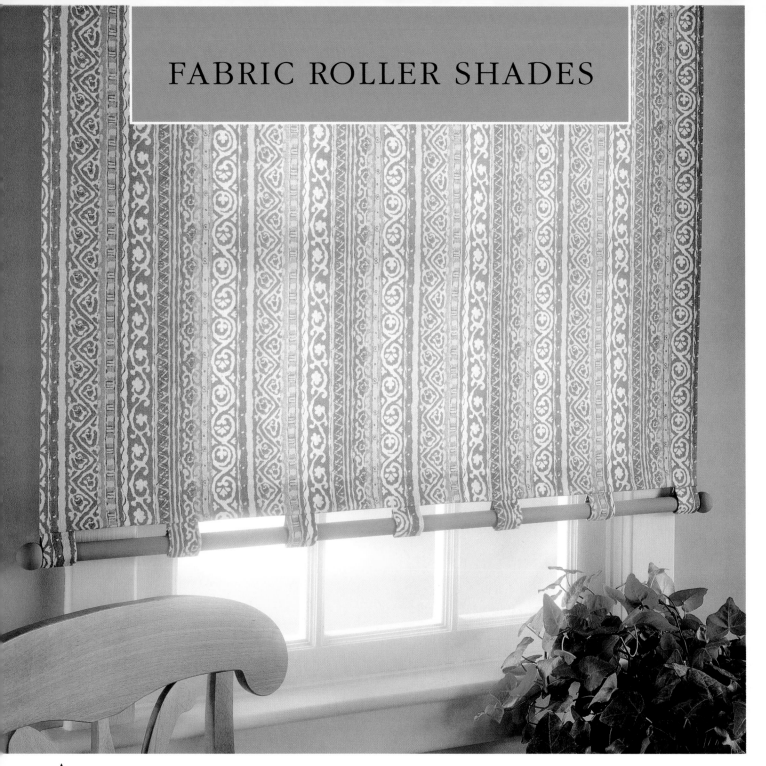

A fabric roller shade is a very affordable window treatment, because it requires only enough fabric to cover the window and the hardware cost is minimal. For a basic roller shade, fuse a simple hem at the lower edge. Or, for a distinctive look, add tabs and a decorative rod with finials, shape the lower edge, or make a lace cutout.

Pulley-system shades are easily raised and lowered, to the desired height by pulling a cord on the side of the shade. These shades can be made from kits, complete with fusible shade backing that controls light and gives a uniform white appearance from the outside of the house. Depending on the brand of the kit, the shade fabric is attached either to an adjustable metal roller or to a cardboard roller that is cut to size.

For an inside-mounted shade, the window frame must be deep enough to accommodate the installed roller. If this is not the case, the shade can be installed as an outside mount, either to the front of the window frame or on the wall just beyond the frame. Install the brackets and mount the roller before cutting the fabric, to determine the exact finished width and length of the shade. Follow the manufacturer's instructions to determine the size of the roller and install the shade.

Avoid heavily glazed fabrics, such as chintz, because these fabrics do not bond well to the fusible backing. Also some fabrics with stain-resistant and water-repellent finishes may not bond well. Before using these fabrics, make a test sample to check the bond.

MATERIALS

- Pulley-system roller shade kit that includes fusible shade backing.
- Lightweight to mediumweight fabric.
- Fusible web, ⅜" (1 cm) wide, if not included in shade kit.
- Liquid fray preventer and small brush; masking tape or vinyl tape.
- ⅞" (2.2 cm) wooden dowel, for roller shade with a tabbed hem; finials, for outside-mounted shade with tabs, optional.
- Paint or stain and clear acrylic finish, for finishing the dowel and finials.

CUTTING DIRECTIONS

Install the mounting brackets and roller, and measure the roller as on page 26, step 1, to determine the finished width of the shade. Steam-press the fabric thoroughly to prevent shrinking. Using a T-square to ensure perfectly squared corners, cut the fabric 2" (5 cm) wider than the desired finished width of the shade and 12" (30.5 cm) longer than the desired finished length.

Cut the fusible backing 1" (2.5 cm) wider than the desired finished width of the shade and 12" (30.5 cm) longer than desired finished length, cutting perfectly squared corners.

TWO WAYS TO HANG A ROLLER SHADE

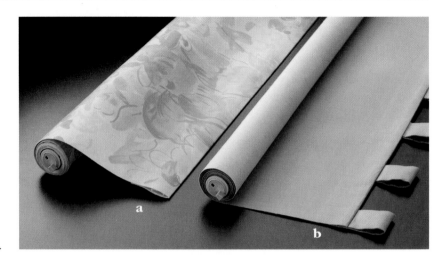

Determine how you will hang the roller shade before you begin. If the top of the shade will be visible when the shade is mounted, install the shade so it rolls off the front of the roller with the right side of the shade facing out as it wraps around the roller **(a).** If the roller will be concealed by a valance or cornice, the shade can be installed so it rolls off the back of the roller with the wrong side of the shade facing out as it wraps around the roller **(b);** this allows you to install the shade closer to the window for better energy efficiency and light control.

HOW TO MAKE A BASIC PULLEY-SYSTEM ROLLER SHADE

1 Install shade brackets, roller, pulley, and end plug at window according to the manufacturer's instructions. Measure the roller from inside edge of end plug to inside edge of pulley to determine finished width of the shade. Cut fabric and backing (page 25).

2 Fuse the backing to wrong side of fabric, centering it on the width of the fabric; fabric extends ½" (1.3 cm) beyond backing on each side. Use a press cloth, and follow manufacturer's instructions.

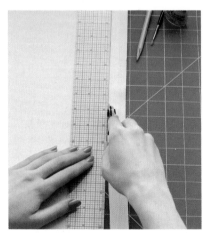

3 Mark finished width of shade on backing. Cut on marked lines. Apply liquid fray preventer to edges sparingly, using small brush.

4 Turn under 2" (5 cm) at lower edge, for hem pocket. Fuse in place at top of hem pocket, using fusible web.

5 Mark a line down the center of the roller by holding the roller firmly in place on a table; lay a marker flat on the table and slide it down the length of the roller.

6 Attach shade to roller by taping upper edge in place along marked line, from inner edge of pulley to inner edge of end plug. As shown opposite, tape shade to roller right side up if the shade will fall around front of the roller; tape shade to roller wrong side up if the shade will fall around the back of the roller.

7 Trim hem stick to fit pocket at lower hem; slide into pocket. Mount roller shade into brackets.

HOW TO MAKE A ROLLER SHADE WITH A TABBED HEM

1 Cut desired number of tabs from fabric, 3" (7.5 cm) wide and 4½" (11.5 cm) long. Follow steps 1 to 3, opposite; cut 2" (5 cm) facing strip from lower edge of fused shade.

2 Fold long edges of tab to the center, wrong sides together; press. Fuse in place, using ⅜" (1 cm) strip of fusible web. Repeat for all tabs.

3 Fold the tabs in half; pin to the lower edge of shade on right side, with the outer edges of the end tabs even with the outer edge of shade and spacing tabs evenly. Baste in place.

4 Pin facing to lower edge of shade, right sides together, matching raw edges and hemmed ends. Stitch ⅜" (1 cm) seam through all layers. Turn facing to wrong side; fuse in place at upper edge and ends of facing, using fusible web.

5 Cut dowel ⅛" (3 mm) shorter than finished width of the shade. Paint dowel and finials; or apply stain and clear finish. Insert the dowel into tabs. Attach finials. Secure with thumbtacks on back sides of the first and last tabs. Mount and install the roller shade as above, steps 5 and 6.

HOW TO MAKE A ROLLER SHADE WITH A LACE CUTOUT

1 Follow steps 1 through 4, page 26. Pin lace appliqué to shade fabric, right sides up in desired location. Stitch around outer edge of appliqué, using short, narrow zigzag stitch. (Contrasting thread was used to show detail.)

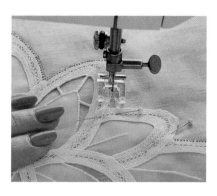

2 Trim away fabric under appliqué about ⅛" (3 mm) away from stitches, taking care not to cut the appliqué. Complete shade as in steps 5 to 7, pages 26 and 27.

HOW TO MAKE A ROLLER SHADE WITH A SHAPED HEM

1 Determine finished width of shade as in step 1, page 26. On paper, draw desired symmetrical shape for lower edge of shade. Cut shade fabric as on page 25; cut lining, if desired. Cut fabric for facing 1½" (3.8 cm) wider than finished width of shade; the cut length of facing is 5" to 7" (12.5 to 18 cm), depending on the depth of the shaped design.

2 Turn under and press ¾" (2 cm) on sides of the shade fabric and facing; fuse in place, using a ¾" (2 cm) strip of fusible web.

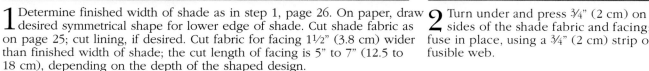

3 Trace the shape for the lower edge of the shade onto wrong side of the facing strip, with longest points of the design ½" (1.3 cm) from the lower edge of the facing. Pin facing strip to the shade fabric, right sides together, aligning the sides and lower edges.

4 Stitch along the marked design line. Trim excess fabric at the lower edge within ¼" (6 mm) of stitching line. Clip to stitching on the curves, and trim corners. Turn the facing to wrong side of the shade; press. Fuse the upper and side edges of facing in place, using ⅜" (1 cm) strip of fusible web.

5 Pin-mark upper edge of facing on sides of shade. Mark line on front of shade, 1½" (3.8 cm) above pin marks, using chalk. Fold shade wrong sides together along marked line; press and pin. Stitch 1½" (3.8 cm) from pressed fold, to make hem-stick pocket. Press pocket toward lower edge of shade.

6 Apply decorative trim to lower edge, if desired, using fabric glue or hand stitching. Wrap ends of the trim to wrong side of the shade; secure. Complete shade as in steps 5 to 7, pages 26 and 27.

STITCHED-TUCK ROMAN SHADES

Stitched-tuck Roman shades have a neat, clean-lined appearance. They raise and lower easily, offering light control and privacy. They allow as much of the window to be exposed as desired and provide complete coverage when needed. And, because they require only a minimal amount of fabric, they are also an economical window treatment.

The shade has horizontal tucks stitched at evenly spaced intervals with alternate tucks stitched toward the front, then toward the back. When the shade is raised, the fabric folds along the tucks accordion-style. To help the shade hang smoothly, a weight bar is inserted into the hem at the lower edge. The depth of the lower hem is equal to the distance between the tucks.

This shade is attached to a mounting board and may be installed as either an outside mount or an inside mount. For an outside mount, the mounting board is installed above the window. For an inside mount, it is installed at the top of the window, inside the frame; the window frame must be deep enough to accommodate a 1 × 1 mounting board.

CALCULATING THE TUCKS & SPACES

You may choose the distance between the stitched tucks according to the look you want; a spacing of about 4" (10 cm) between the tucks is attractive. Before you cut the fabric, it is helpful to sketch the Roman shade as shown on page 32, indicating the number of tucks and spaces.

For an outside-mounted shade, if the estimated finished length of the shade is not evenly divisible by the desired space between the tucks, the measurement for the length can be rounded up until it is. For example, if you would like 4" (10 cm) spaces between the tucks and the estimated finished length is 45" (115 cm), you can round up the measurement to a 48" (122 cm) finished length, which is divisible by four. This allows for a 4" (10 cm) space between each of the tucks, a 4" (10 cm) space at the top, and a 4" (10 cm) hem depth at the bottom of the shade, for a total of 12 spaces.

Sometimes the length of the shade cannot be adjusted, as for an inside-mounted shade that must fit within the window frame. In this case, the spacing between the tucks can be changed. For example, if the estimated space between the tucks is 4" (10 cm) and the desired finished length of the shade is 45" (115 cm), you may have ten 4½" (11.5 cm) spaces; this includes the spaces between the tucks, the space at the top of the shade, and the space for the hem depth at the bottom. Or you can have nine

5" (12.5 cm) spaces, including the top space and the hem depth.

When cutting the fabric and the lining, it is important to make square cuts so the finished shade will hang straight. Use a carpenter's square for accuracy in cutting.

INSTALLING THE SHADE

For a professional appearance, the mounting board is covered with fabric (page 16). On an outside mount, use fabric that matches the shade, because the covered board is visible on the sides.

For an outside-mounted shade, a 1 × 2 mounting board is used. Depending on whether you mount the board flat or on edge, it can be used for either a ¾" or 1½" (2 or 3.8 cm) projection, as shown on page 17.

For an outside mount with a 1½" (3.8 cm) projection, the mounting board is secured to the window frame or wall using angle irons. If you are securing the board to the wall, screw the angle irons into wall studs, whenever possible, using flat-head screws. If it is necessary to install angle irons between wall studs into drywall or plaster, use molly bolts or toggle bolts to ensure a secure installation.

For an outside mount with a ¾" (2 cm) projection, or for an inside mount, angle irons are not needed; the board is screwed directly into the window frame or wall (page 17). A 1 × 2 board is used for an outside mount, and a 1 × 1 board is used for an inside mount.

HOW A ROMAN SHADE WORKS

Back view shows the mechanics of a Roman shade. The shade is raised by pulling on the draw cord, causing the shade to fold in accordion pleats. The cords are strung through the rows of rings, then along the screw eyes in the mounting board at the top.

MAKING A SKETCH OF THE STITCHED-TUCK ROMAN SHADE

1 Draw sketch, indicating correct number of tucks and spaces. Label sketch with measurements of the finished length and spaces. Blue lines indicate back tucks, and red lines indicate front tucks.

2 Label the sketch with measurements for the finished width and the placement of the rings on the shade. The rings are positioned along the back tucks, starting 1" (2.5 cm) from the side edges and spacing remaining rows of rings evenly 8" to 12" (20.5 to 30.5 cm) apart across the width of the shade. The placement of the screw eyes on the mounting board is directly above the rings.

MATERIALS

- Decorator fabric.
- Lining fabric.
- Fusible web, ½" (1.3 cm) wide.
- ½" (1.3 cm) plastic rings.
- Shade cord; awning cleat.
- 1 × 2 mounting board for an outside mount or 1 × 1 board for an inside mount, cut to length as determined below.

- Screw eyes, number equal to the number of rings across width of shade.
- One ⅜" (1 cm) brass rod or weight bar, cut ½" (1.3 cm) shorter than shade width.
- Angle irons, 1½" (3.8 cm) long, and flat-head wood screws, for installing an outside-mounted shade.

- Molly bolts or toggle bolts, if installing angle irons for an outside-mounted shade into drywall or plaster rather than directly into wall studs.
- 8 × 1½" (3.8 cm) round-head screws, for installing an inside-mounted shade.
- Drill and drill bit; staple gun and staples.

CUTTING DIRECTIONS

Decide where the shade will be mounted. Determine the finished length of the shade from the top of the mounting board to either the sill or ½" (1.3 cm) below the bottom of the apron. Divide the desired space between the tucks into the finished length of the shade; if necessary, round the number up or down to the nearest whole number. This is the number of spaces, including the space at the top of the shade and the hem depth at the bottom.

Then divide the number of spaces into the finished length of the shade; this gives you the exact space between the tucks and the hem depth. There is one less tuck in the shade than there are spaces.

Determine the finished width of the shade. For an outside mount, the shade should extend at least 1" (2.5 cm) beyond the window frame on each side. For an inside mount, measure across the window, inside the frame. To allow for any variance in the width of the frame, measure it across the top, middle, and bottom. The finished width should be ⅛" (3 mm) less than the shortest of these three measurements.

Cut the fabric to the desired finished length of the shade plus twice the hem depth, plus ¾" (2 cm) for each tuck, plus the projection of the mounting board. Also add 2" (5 cm), to allow for any shrinkage in the length that

results from multiple rows of stitching; after the shade is sewn, any excess length is trimmed off at the top.

The cut width of the shade fabric is 3" (7.5 cm) wider than the finished width of the shade. If more than one fabric width is required for the shade, use one complete width for a center panel; seam equal partial widths on each side, matching the pattern in the fabric.

Cut the lining to the same length as the outer fabric minus twice the depth of the hem at the bottom. The cut width of the lining is equal to the finished width of the shade; if necessary, seam equal partial widths on each side of a center panel, as for the shade fabric.

For an inside-mounted shade, cut a 1 × 1 mounting board ½" (1.3 cm) shorter than the inside measurement of the window frame. This ensures that the mounting board will fit inside the frame after it is covered with fabric. For an outside-mounted shade, cut a 1 × 2 board to the desired finished width of the shade; this measurement should be at least 2" (5 cm) longer than the outside measurement of the window frame.

Cut the fabric to cover the mounting board, with the width of the fabric equal to the distance around the board plus 1" (2.5 cm) and the length of the fabric equal to the length of the board plus 3" (7.5 cm).

HOW TO MAKE A STITCHED-TUCK ROMAN SHADE

1 Seam fabric widths together, if necessary; cut fabric (opposite). Stabilize the side edges by applying liquid fray preventer, or finish the edges, using overlock or zigzag stitch. Press under 1½" (3.8 cm) on each side, for the hems.

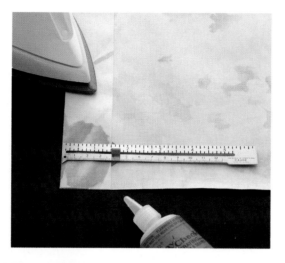

2 Place shade fabric facedown on flat surface; place the lining on shade fabric, wrong sides together, with the upper edges matching. Place lining under side hems up to foldline.

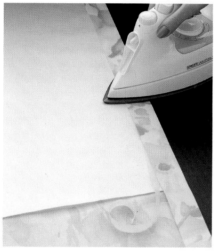

3 Fuse the side hems in place over the lining, using ½" (1.3 cm) strips of fusible web.

4 Press under an amount equal to the hem depth at lower edge of shade fabric; then press under again, to make double-fold hem. Pin in place. Stitch along upper fold.

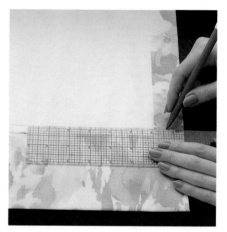

5 Place shade fabric facedown on flat surface. On the lining, mark a line for the first back tuck, ⅜" (1 cm) above stitched upper fold of hem.

6 Mark lines on the lining for remaining back tucks; to determine distance between the marked lines, multiply calculated space between each front and back tuck by two, and add 1½" (3.8 cm). For example, mark the lines 9½" (24.3 cm) apart for a shade with 4" (10 cm) spaces between the front and back tucks. This allows for stitching the ⅜" (1 cm) tucks.

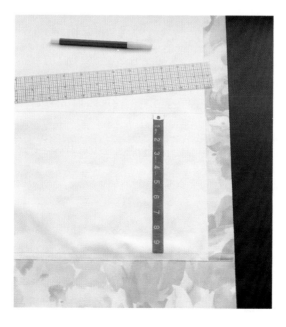

7 Pin lining to shade fabric along the marked lines. Press shade along first marked line, right sides together. Stitch ⅜" (1 cm) from fold, to stitch back tuck; repeat for remaining back tucks. For the first tuck, it may be helpful to use a zipper foot, because the stitching line is even with fold of hem.

(Continued)

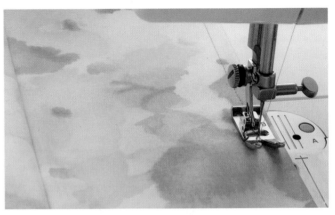

8 Fold shade, wrong sides together, aligning the first two back tucks **(a)**. From the right side of the shade, press the fold for first front tuck **(b)**; pin.

9 Fold and press the remaining front tucks. Stitch all front tucks 3⁄8" (1 cm) from folds.

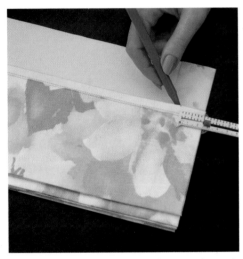

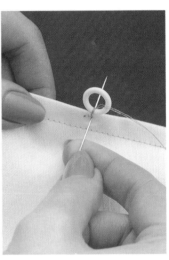

10 Fold shade, stacking front tucks and back tucks. Mark placement for rings on back tucks, beginning 1" (2.5 cm) from side edges and spacing remaining rows of rings evenly 8" to 12" (20.5 to 30.5 cm) apart across the width of the shade.

11 **Attaching the rings by machine.** Attach rings at marks, placing the fold under the presser foot with ring next to fold. Set zigzag stitch at widest setting; set stitch length at 0. Stitch over the ring, securing it with about eight stitches. Then stitch in place for two or three stitches, with stitch width and length set at 0; this secures threads.

11 **Attaching the rings by hand.** Tack rings by hand, using a double strand of thread, stitching in place through both fabric layers for four or five stitches.

12 Slide weight bar into hem at lower edge of the shade. Stitch the side openings closed.

13 Cover the mounting board (page 16). Place the shade facedown on flat surface. Pulling the fabric taut, measure from the lower edge of the shade to the desired finished length; mark a line on lining fabric. This may change the upper space of the shade somewhat, but ensures that the shade is the correct length.

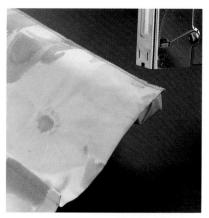

14 **Inside mount.** Place 1 × 1 mounting board on shade, aligning the edge of board with the marked line. Mark fabric along opposite edge of board, to mark the distance of projection away from first line. Cut on the second marked line.

14 **Outside mount.** Place a 1 × 2 mounting board on shade, aligning edge of board with marked line. For 1½" (3.8 cm) projection **(a)**, place board flat on table; for ¾" (2 cm) projection **(b)**, stand board on edge. Mark fabric and cut on the marked line as in step 14, left.

15 Finish upper edges of fabric and lining by stitching layers together, using overlock or zigzag stitch. Position upper front edge of mounting board along first marked line; finished edge of shade extends to back edge of board. Staple shade to top of board.

16 Install the screw eyes on underside of mounting board, aligning them with rows of rings.

17 Decide whether the draw cord will hang on the left or right side of shade. String the first row of shade, opposite the draw side. Run the cord through rings, from bottom to top and across the top through the screw eyes; extend the cord about three-fourths of the way down the outer edge of shade, for the draw cord.

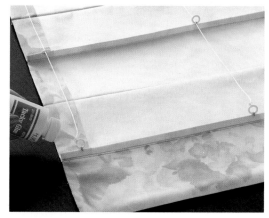

18 Cut and tie cord for first row securely at bottom ring. String the remaining rows, running cord through each succeeding row of rings and through screw eyes; cut and tie each cord at bottom ring. Apply fabric glue to knots, to prevent them from fraying or becoming untied.

19 Mount shade to wall or window frame (pages 16 and 17). Adjust length of cords, with shade lowered so the tension on each cord is equal. Tie cords together just below screw eye. Braid cords to the desired length. Knot end of braided cord.

20 Screw awning cleat into window frame or wall. When the shade is raised, wrap the cord around awning cleat.

BANDED ROMAN SHADES WITH A CENTER DRAW

A banded Roman shade that draws up the center requires only a minimal amount of fabric, but is a stylish treatment that provides privacy and light control. When raised, the shade gathers up the center, and the sides curve gracefully. Banding along the sides and lower edge adds interest to the shade.

Select a lightweight to mediumweight fabric that does not wrinkle easily, to create soft gathers when the shade is raised, yet maintain a wrinkle-free, smooth appearance when it is lowered.

Line the Roman shade, if desired, using lightweight to mediumweight lining fabric. For an unlined shade with a light, airy look, you may use a semisheer shade fabric, with opaque fabric for the banding.

MATERIALS

- Lightweight to mediumweight decorator fabric.
- Lining fabric, optional.
- ½" (1.3 cm) plastic rings.
- Two screw eyes.
- Shade cord; awning cleat; small drapery pull.
- 1 × 2 mounting board for an outside mount or 1 × 1 board for an inside mount, cut to length as determined on page 32.
- Angle irons, 1½" (3.8 cm) long, and flat-head wood screws, for installing an outside-mounted shade.
- Molly bolts or toggle bolts, if installing the angle irons for an outside-mounted shade into drywall or plaster rather than directly into wall studs.
- #8 × 1½" (3.8 cm) round-head screws, for installing an inside-mounted shade.
- Drill and drill bit; staple gun and staples.

CUTTING DIRECTIONS

Decide where the shade will be mounted. Determine the finished length of the shade from the top of the mounting board to either the sill or ½" (1.3 cm) below the bottom of the apron. Determine the finished width of the shade. For an outside mount, the shade should extend at least 1" (2.5 cm) beyond the window frame on each side. For an inside mount, measure across the window, inside the frame.

Cut the fabric to the finished length of the shade plus the projection of the mounting board plus ½" (1.3 cm). The cut width of the shade is equal to the finished width plus 1" (2.5 cm). If more than one width of the fabric is required for the shade, use one complete width for the center panel; seam equal partial widths to each side of the center panel, to achieve the necessary width. If a lining is desired, cut the lining fabric to the same length and width as the outer fabric.

Cut the fabric strips for the banded edges, with the cut width of the strips 1" (2.5 cm) wider than the desired finished width of the band. For the side bands, cut two fabric strips equal to the cut length of the shade. For the lower band, cut one fabric strip equal to the cut width of the shade.

HOW TO MAKE A BANDED ROMAN SHADE
WITH A CENTER DRAW

1 Seam fabric widths together, if necessary. For a lined shade, pin the lining to the outer fabric, wrong sides together, matching the raw edges; machine-baste ⅜" (1 cm) from raw edges.

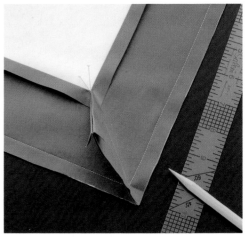

2 Press under ½" (1.3 cm) on one long edge of one side band. Pin band to the shade panel, with right side of the band to wrong side of the panel. Stitch a ½" (1.3 cm) seam, stopping ½" (1.3 cm) from the lower edge. Repeat for the band on the opposite side.

3 Press under ½" (1.3 cm) on one long edge of lower band. Pin to the lower edge of the shade, with right side of the band to wrong side of panel. Stitch a ½" (1.3 cm) seam, starting and stopping ½" (1.3 cm) from the side edges.

4 Mark band for mitering, placing pins at inner corner as shown.

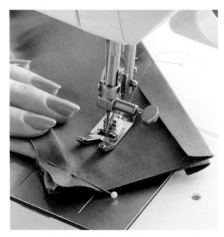

5 Stitch miters from the pin marks at inner corner to the end of stitching at outer corner; take care not to catch shade panel in stitching.

6 Trim mitered seams to ½" (1.3 cm), and press open. Trim the corners diagonally.

7 Press the seams open by pressing seam allowance of band toward band, using tip of iron.

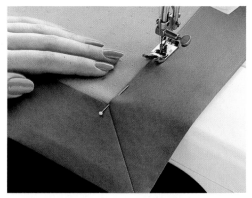

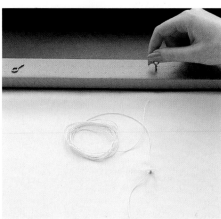

8 Turn the band to the right side of shade; press band, with seamline on the outer edge of the shade. Pin the band in place. Stitch around the band, close to inside fold. Finish upper edge of shade, using zigzag or overlock stitch.

9 Fold shade in half, right sides together. On the center fold, mark the placement for the rings, spaced evenly 4" to 6" (10 to 15 cm) apart; the ring at bottom of shade is to be positioned at stitching line on upper edge of the lower band, and the space above top ring should be equal to the other spaces plus the projection of the mounting board.

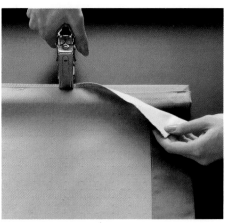

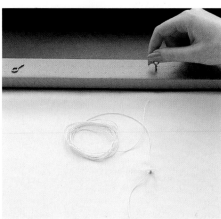

10 Hand-stitch rings in place with several small, vertical stitches; if shade is lined, catch outer fabric in stitching.

11 Cover mounting board (page 16). Staple shade to mounting board, aligning the upper edge of shade to the back edge of board. For a 1½" (3.8 cm) projection, place board flat on table; for a ¾" (2 cm) projection, stand the board on edge.

12 Install screw eye on underside of mounting board, aligned above the row of rings. Determine whether draw cord will hang on the right or left side of the shade; install a second screw eye ½" (1.3 cm) from the corresponding end of board.

13 Place shade facedown on flat surface. Run the cord through the rings, from bottom to top, through the screw eyes; extend cord about three-fourths of the way down the outer edge of the shade. Cut and tie cord at the lower ring. Apply fabric glue to knot.

14 Mount the shade to wall or window frame (pages 16 and 17). Adjust the length of cord, if necessary; attach drapery pull to the end of cord. Screw awning cleat into the window frame or wall; when shade is raised, wrap the cord around awning cleat.

HOBBLED ROMAN SHADES

Hobbled Roman shades are constructed with soft horizontal folds that add interest and dimension. Rings are stitched to the wrong side of the shade through vertical rows of twill tape. Because the shade is visually interrupted by the folds, best results are achieved with plain fabrics or all-over prints.

The shade is attached to a mounting board and can be installed as either an inside or outside mount (pages 16 and 17). A weight bar inserted into the lower hem helps the shade hang smoothly.

CALCULATING THE RING SPACING

The distance between rings can vary, depending on the desired look for the shade. A distance of 4" (10 cm) between rings is attractive for most windows; because the length of fabric in each fold is equal to twice the distance between the rings, this requires 8" (20.5 cm) of fabric for each fold. It is helpful to diagram the shade as shown below, drawing in the spaces between the rings and the number of folds.

For an outside-mounted shade, if the estimated finished length of the shade is not evenly divisible by the desired space between the rings, the measurement for the finished length can be rounded up until it is, provided there is the necessary wall space above the window for mounting. For example, if you would like 4" (10 cm) spaces between the rings and the estimated finished length is 45" (115 cm), you can round up the measurement to a 48" (122 cm) finished length, which is divisible by four. This allows for a 4" (10 cm) hem depth, ten 4" (10 cm) spaces between the rings, and 4" (10 cm) between the top ring and the top of the mounting board.

If the length of the shade cannot be adjusted, as is the case with an inside-mounted shade that must fit within the window frame, the spacing between the rings can be adjusted. For example, a shade measuring 45" (115 cm) in length can be constructed with a 4½" (11.5 cm) hem depth and nine 4½" (11.5 cm) spaces, including the space between the top ring and the top of the mounting board. Another alternative is a 5" (12.5 cm) hem depth and eight 5" (12.5 cm) spaces.

MAKING A DIAGRAM OF THE SHADE

1 Diagram side view of the hobbled shade, including the hem, the correct number of spaces between rings, and length of fabric in the folds. Label the finished length of the shade, the distance between rings, and the hem depth. The hem depth and the distance between top ring and top of board are equal to the distance between rings.

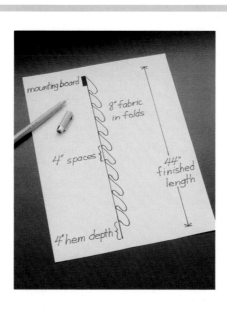

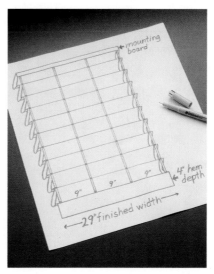

2 Diagram the shade from the back, indicating the number of vertical rows of twill tape and rings, and the spacing between the rows. Place one row 1" (2.5 cm) from each side, and evenly space remaining rows 8" to 12" (20.5 to 30.5 cm) apart across the shade.

- Decorator fabric.
- Lining fabric.
- Fusible web, ½" (1.3 cm) wide.
- ½" (1.3 cm) plastic rings.
- ½" (1.3 cm) polyester twill tape; to determine yardage needed, multiply number of rows by finished shade length.
- 1 × 2 mounting board, cut to length as determined on page 16.

- Screw eyes, one for each row of twill tape and rings.
- Shade cord.
- Awning cleat.
- Weight bar, ¼" (6 mm) to ⅜" (1 cm) in diameter; wood dowel, aluminum rod, or brass rod may be used.
- 1½" (3.8 cm) angle irons with flat-head screws, for installing an outside-mounted shade.

- 8 × 2½" (6.5 cm) flat-head screws, for installing outside-mounted valance into wall studs; or molly bolts or toggle anchors, for installing outside-mounted shade into drywall or plaster.
- 8 × 1½" (3.8 cm) round-head screws, for installing an inside-mounted shade.
- Staple gun and staples.
- Drill and ⅛" drill bit.

CUTTING DIRECTIONS

Determine the finished length of the shade from the top of the mounting board to either the sill or ½" (1.3 cm) below the bottom of the apron.

Determine the finished width of the shade. For an outside mount, the shade should extend at least 1" (2.5 cm) beyond the window frame on each side. For an inside mount, measure the inside of the window frame from side to side at the top, middle, and bottom; subtract ⅛" (3 mm) from the narrowest of these measurements for the finished width of the shade.

The cut length of the shade fabric is equal to twice the finished length of the shade plus the hem depth plus the projection of the mounting board (page 16). The cut width of the shade fabric is equal to the finished width of the

shade plus 3" (7.5 cm). If more than one width of fabric is needed for the shade, use a complete width for the center of the shade and seam equal partial widths to each side.

Cut the lining to the cut length of the shade fabric minus twice the hem depth. The cut width of the lining is equal to the finished width of the shade.

Determine the number of rows of twill tape needed; steam-press the tape to preshrink it, and cut each piece to the length of the finished shade.

Cut the weight bar ½" (1.3 cm) shorter than the finished width of the shade.

Cut the fabric to cover the mounting board.

HOW TO MAKE A HOBBLED ROMAN SHADE

1 Seam fabric widths together, if necessary; trim to the cut width determined above. Repeat for lining fabric. Stabilize the side edges by applying liquid fray preventer or by finishing the edges, using overlock or zigzag stitch. Press under 1½" (3.8 cm) on each side, for the hems.

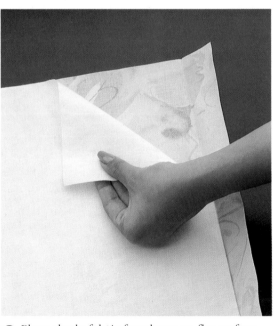

2 Place shade fabric facedown on flat surface. Place lining on the shade fabric, wrong sides together, with upper edges matching. Place lining under the side hems, up to foldlines.

3 Fuse the side hems over the lining, using ½" (1.3 cm) strips of fusible web.

4 Press under an amount equal to the hem depth at lower edge of shade fabric; then press under again, to make double-fold hem. Pin in place.

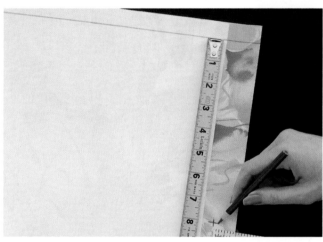

5 Mark a line across top of shade to indicate projection of mounting board. Mark placement for rings in first vertical row, 1" (2.5 cm) from side of shade, with top mark 8" (20 cm) below marked line for projection and with bottom mark at upper edge of hem. Space marks a distance apart equal to twice the distance between rings as calculated on page 41; repeat for opposite side.

6 Mark placement for rings in the first horizontal row at upper edge of hem, spacing rows as determined in your diagram of shade (page 41). Continue marking placement for all remaining rings. Pin the lining to shade fabric at each ring placement mark.

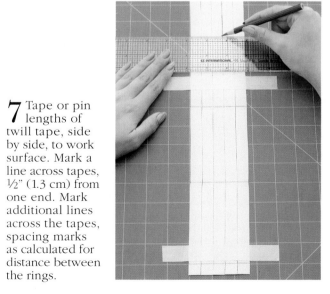

7 Tape or pin lengths of twill tape, side by side, to work surface. Mark a line across tapes, ½" (1.3 cm) from one end. Mark additional lines across the tapes, spacing marks as calculated for distance between the rings.

8 Insert ½" (1.3 cm) ends of tapes under top edge of hem up to first line, centering one tape at each ring placement mark; pin in place. Stitch hem in place, catching tapes in stitching.

(Continued)

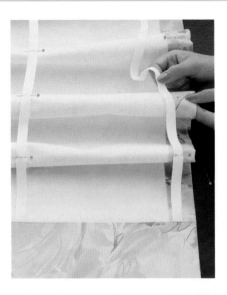

9 Pin the twill tapes to ring marks, beginning at the bottom of the shade, centering the tapes on the ring marks and pinning through all the layers.

10 Attaching rings by machine. Set zigzag stitch at the widest setting; set stitch length at 0. Fold shade, right sides together, along first horizontal row of pins. Place ring next to folded edge. At center of twill tape, stitch over the ring and folded edge with about eight stitches. Secure the stitches by stitching in place for two or three stitches, with the stitch width and length set at 0. Repeat for remaining horizontal rows.

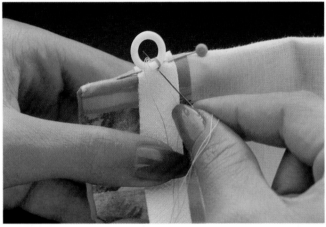

10 Attaching rings by hand. Tack rings by hand, using double strand of thread, stitching in place through the tape, lining, and shade fabric for four or five stitches.

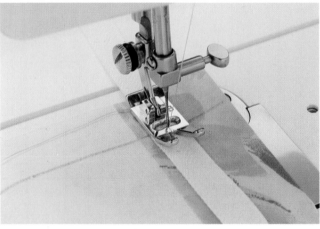

11 Tack the tapes in place at top of shade, matching the last marks on the tapes to marked lines on the shade; do not stitch rings at the top marks.

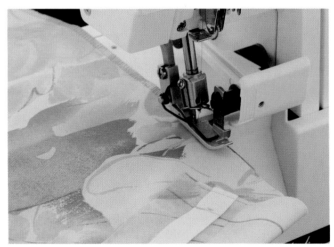

12 Trim excess tapes even with upper edge of shade, and secure ends to shade. Finish upper edge of the shade, using overlock or zigzag stitch; catch the ends of the tapes in the stitching.

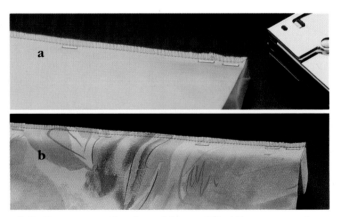

13 Cover mounting board (page 16). Align upper edge of shade to back top edge of mounting board. Staple in place, stapling through the tapes and between them. For inside-mounted shade or outside-mounted shade with 1½" (3.8 cm) projection **(a),** shade is stapled to wide side of the board. For outside-mounted shade with ¾" (2 cm) projection **(b),** shade is stapled to narrow side of board.

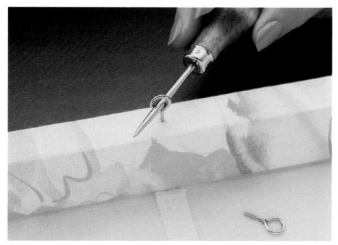

14 Install screw eyes on underside of mounting board, aligning them to rows of rings. For easy installation of screw eyes, use awl or screwdriver as shown.

15 Slide the weight bar into hem at lower edge of shade. Hand-stitch ends of hem closed.

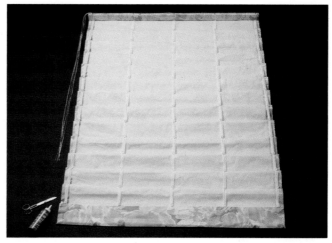

16 Place the shade facedown on a flat surface. Decide whether the draw cord will hang on left or right side of shade. String first row of the shade, opposite the draw side. Run cord through the rings from bottom to top and across the shade through screw eyes; extend cord about three-fourths of the way down the draw side of the shade.

17 Cut and tie the cord for first row securely at bottom ring. String the remaining rows, running the cord through each succeeding row of rings and through the screw eyes; cut and tie each cord at the bottom ring. Apply fabric glue to the knots, to prevent them from fraying or becoming untied.

18 Mount the shade to wall or window frame (page 17). Adjust length of the cords, with shade lowered so the tension on each cord is equal. Tie the cords together just below screw eye. Braid cords to the desired length; knot.

19 Screw awning cleat into window frame or wall. When shade is raised, wrap the cord around awning cleat.

SLATTED
ROMAN SHADES

Slatted Roman shades have a sleek, contemporary look. The flat surface of the shade is interrupted by horizontal pockets that carry narrow wooden slats. Because the slats also give dimensional stability to the shade, only three rows of rings are needed on the back of the shade. For best results, the width of the shade should not exceed 50" (127 cm). As with other styles of Roman shades, the slatted shade is attached to a mounting board and can be installed inside or outside the window frame.

CALCULATING THE POCKET SPACING

It is helpful to make a diagram of the shade, indicating the number of pockets and spaces and labeling the measurements as shown below. The slat pockets and the hem pocket all have a depth of 1½" (3.8 cm). The pockets are evenly spaced, 8" to 10" (20.5 to 25.5 cm) apart, with 9" (23 cm) being most desirable.

For an outside-mounted shade, if the estimated finished length of the shade is not evenly divisible by the desired space between the pockets, the measurement for the finished length can be rounded up until it is, provided there is the necessary wall space above the window for mounting.

If the length of the shade cannot be adjusted, as is the case with an inside-mounted shade that must fit within the window frame, the space between the pockets must be calculated to fit the length. To determine the exact measurement for the spaces, first subtract the 1½" (3.8 cm) hem depth from the finished length. Then divide the remainder by 9, and round this number up or down to the nearest whole number to determine the number of spaces. Next, divide the finished length minus the 1½" (3.8 cm) hem depth by the number of spaces to determine the exact space measurement.

MAKING A DIAGRAM OF THE SHADE

Diagram shade, indicating the necessary number of slat pockets and spaces. Also indicate the hem depth of 1½" (3.8 cm). Label the measurement of all spaces as calculated above. Check to be sure that the total measurement calculated equals the desired finished length of the shade.

MATERIALS

- Decorator fabric.
- Lining fabric.
- Fusible web, ½" (1.3 cm) wide.
- ½" (1.3 cm) plastic rings.
- ⅞" (2.2 cm) wooden slats, such as the slats used for roller shade hem pockets.
- 1 × 2 mounting board, cut to length as determined on page 16.
- Three screw eyes.
- Shade cord.
- Awning cleat.
- 1½" (3.8 cm) angle irons with flat-head screws, for installing an outside-mounted shade.
- 8 × 2½" (6.5 cm) flat-head screws, for installing outside-mounted shade into wall studs; or molly bolts or toggle anchors, for installing outside-mounted shade into drywall or plaster.
- 8 × 1½" (3.8 cm) round-head screws, for installing an inside-mounted shade.
- Staple gun and staples.
- Drill and ⅛" drill bit.

CUTTING DIRECTIONS

Determine the finished length of the shade from the top of the mounting board to either the sill or ½" (1.3 cm) below the bottom of the apron.

Determine the finished width of the shade. For an outside mount, the shade should extend at least 1" (2.5 cm) beyond the window frame on each side. For an inside mount, measure the inside of the window frame, from side to side, at the top, middle, and bottom; subtract ⅛" (3 mm) from the narrowest of these measurements for the finished width of the shade.

Cut the shade fabric to the finished length of the shade plus 2" (5 cm) for the turn-under and hem allowance plus 3" (7.5 cm) for each slat pocket plus 4" (10 cm). The cut width is equal to the finished width of the shade plus 3" (7.5 cm) for side hems.

Cut the lining 2" (5 cm) shorter than the cut length of the shade fabric. The cut width of the lining is equal to the finished width of the shade.

Cut a wooden slat for each pocket and one for the hem, ½" (1.3 cm) shorter than the finished width of the shade.

Cut the fabric to cover the mounting board (page 16).

HOW TO MAKE A SLATTED ROMAN SHADE

1 Follow steps 1 to 3 on pages 42 and 43. Press under ½" (1.3 cm) at lower edge; then press under 1½" (3.8 cm), to make hem pocket. Stitch close to first fold.

2 Place shade faceup on flat surface. Measure from the lower edge an amount equal to the calculated spacing between pockets plus 3" (7.5 cm). Draw a chalk line parallel to lower edge.

3 Measure up from first marked line the same distance as in step 2, and mark another line. Repeat for each slat pocket.

4 Fold shade, wrong sides together, along first chalk line, keeping the lining and shade fabric together; press. Pin along pressed fold.

5 Repeat step 4 for each marked line. Stitch 1½" (3.8 cm) from foldlines to make slat pockets. Press the pockets toward lower edge of shade.

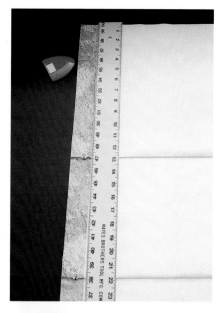

6 Mark placement for rings on wrong side of the shade in three evenly spaced vertical rows, with outer rows 1" (2.5 cm) from the outer edges of the shade. Mark the placement for the bottom rings at upper edge of the hem; mark the placement for remaining rings just under stitching lines. Attach rings by machine or by hand (page 44), keeping slat pockets free.

7 Cover the mounting board (page 16). Place the shade facedown on flat surface. Measure from the lower edge of shade to desired finished length; mark a line on the lining fabric. This may change the length of the top spacing slightly, but ensures that the shade is the correct length.

8 **Inside mount.** Place mounting board flat on shade, aligning lower edge of board to marked line. Mark fabric along opposite edge of board, to mark the distance of the projection away from the first line.

8 **Outside mount.** Place the mounting board on shade, aligning the lower edge of board to marked line. For 1½" (3.8 cm) projection **(a)**, place board flat; for ¾" (2 cm) projection **(b)**, stand board on edge. Mark the fabric as in step 8, left.

9 Cut off excess fabric above second line. Finish upper edge of shade, using overlock or zigzag stitch. Secure shade to the mounting board and install screw eyes as on pages 44 and 45, steps 13 and 14.

10 Slide wooden slats into hem pocket and slat pockets. Hand-stitch ends of pockets closed. Complete the shade as on page 45, steps 16 to 19.

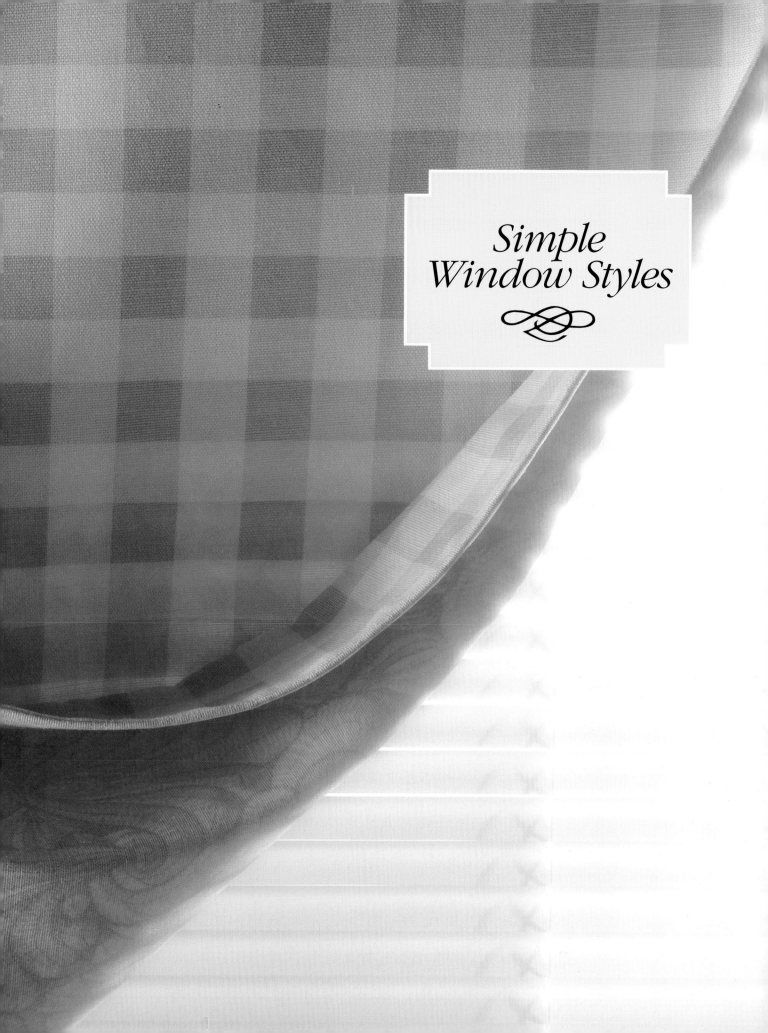

Simple Window Styles

DRAPED WINDOW TREATMENTS

Soft, draping window treatments can be made quickly, using sheer to lightweight reversible fabrics. Since the treatments are made without side hems or seams, it is important to use fabric with neat, narrow selvages. Lace fabrics with finished side edges are also suitable. Though lace is technically not reversible, it usually takes close inspection to distinguish right from wrong sides.

Suitable fabrics may vary in width from 48" to 60" (122 to 152.5 cm). The number of fabric widths needed depends on the width of the window and the style of the treatment. Experiment with inexpensive fabric to determine the number of fabric widths needed.

Several options are available for mounting the window treatment. Hanging the fabric over a decorative rod or pole mounted just above the window frame is the easiest installation method. For a unique look, the fabric can be tied to decorative hooks or knobs mounted on or above the window frame. If the treatment requires tieback holders, simple hidden tenter hooks may be used. A wide selection of decorative holders is also available.

When the treatment is mounted on a pole, the lower edge of

Lace fabric *is hung over a decorative rod and secured at the sides of the window with holdbacks.*

any flat panel will be straight and can therefore fall just below the window frame or sill, or just above the floor, if desired. A treatment tied to knobs or hooks at the top of the window frame will not have a straight lower edge. Plan to have the lower edge of this window treatment style puddle on the floor or hang unevenly 3" to 5" (7.5 to 12.5 cm) below the window frame.

MATERIALS

- Sheer to lightweight, softly draping reversible fabric with neat, narrow selvages or lace with finished edges, 48" to 60" (122 to 153.5 cm) wide; length as determined in cutting directions on pages 54 and 55.

- Decorative rod or pole and mounting brackets; or decorative hooks or knobs for mounting window treatment. Plan three hooks or knobs for first fabric width plus two hooks or knobs for each additional fabric width.

- Tenter hooks or decorative tieback holders.

- Ribbon or cord for tying fabric to knobs or hooks at top of window, or to tieback holders or tenter hooks at sides.

Reversible semisheer fabric is tied to decorative hooks above the window. The front panel is tied in a graceful knot, while the back panel puddles on the floor.

HOW TO INSTALL A DRAPED WINDOW TREATMENT ON HOOKS OR KNOBS

CUTTING DIRECTIONS

Cut each width of fabric with the length equal to twice the desired finished length of the treatment plus 40" (102 cm) for floor puddles and hems. For treatments with free-hanging uneven lower edges, cut each width of fabric with the length equal to twice the desired finished length plus 2" (5 cm) for hems.

Decorative knobs that have screws with a wood thread at one end are suitable for inserting into woodwork. Knobs that have screws without a wood thread **(a)** can be made suitable for inserting into woodwork by replacing the screw with a hanger bolt **(b).** Hanger bolts have a metal thread at one end for inserting into the knob and a wood thread at the opposite end for inserting into the woodwork. To avoid splitting the woodwork, predrill holes before inserting the knobs. Use appropriate anchors if installing hanger bolts into drywall.

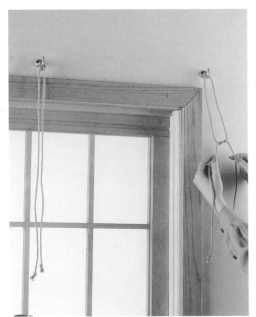

1 Install decorative hooks or knobs on or just above the window frame; position one at each outer edge, with remaining hooks or knobs evenly spaced. Tie a decorative cord or ribbon to each hook or knob, leaving long tails.

2 Hem the cut edges of fabric as in step 1 on page 55. Fold fabric in half, forming two panels, with lower edges even and hem allowances facing the window. Grasp outer edge at fold; tie to hook or knob, 2" to 3" (5 to 7.5 cm) from fold. Repeat at opposite side and again in the center. Repeat for any additional panels. Complete window treatment, using any of the styles on pages 55 through 57.

HOW TO INSTALL A DRAPED WINDOW TREATMENT ON A ROD OR POLE

CUTTING DIRECTIONS

Mount the rod or pole just above the window frame. Cut each width of fabric with the length equal to twice the desired finished length of the treatment plus 40" (102 cm) for floor puddles and hems. For pole-mounted treatments with free-hanging straight lower edges, hang a length of twill tape over the pole to the desired length, with the lower edges even. Cut the fabric 2" (5 cm) longer than the twill tape.

1 Press cut edge under ½" (1.3 cm) twice; stitch to make double-fold hem. Repeat for opposite cut end, pressing fabric in opposite direction.

2 Hang fabric over rod, forming two panels, with lower edges even and hem allowances facing the window. Complete window treatment, using any of the styles below or on pages 56 and 57.

DRAPED WINDOW TREATMENT STYLES

1 **Tiebacks.** Install tieback holders or tenter hooks at the desired height, even with outer edge of window treatment. Grasp outer edge of front fabric panel even with holder.

(Continued)

2 Gather up fabric to opposite edge, at a 45° angle toward the floor. Secure gathered panel to holder. Repeat for the opposite side of back panel, if desired.

1 **Tent flap sides.** Grasp the outer edge of front fabric panel; pull to opposite side, adjusting position of pulled-back edge as desired. Mark wall for placement of tieback holder or tenter hook; mark fabric edge with pin.

2 Install the tieback holder or tenter hook; tie the fabric edge to the holder, using ribbon or cord. Pull back and secure opposite edge of back panel, if desired.

1 **Center knot.** Grasp outer edges of front fabric panel about 18" (46 cm) below desired knot position. Gather up fabric on each side toward the center, gathering upward toward desired knot position.

2 Tie knot in gathered front panel; adjust sides of panel above knot as desired.

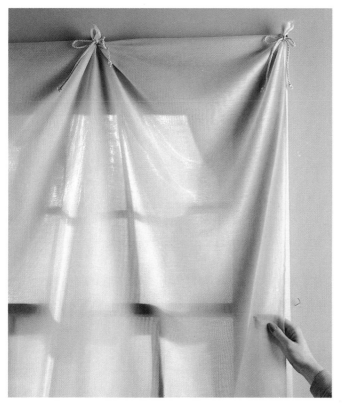

1 **Side knots.** Install tenter hooks at desired knot height, even with outer edge of window treatment. Grasp the outer edge of front fabric panel even with holder.

2 Gather up fabric to opposite edge, gathering at a 45° angle toward floor. Tie knot in panel; secure knot to tenter hook. Make a side knot for opposite side of back panel, if desired.

NO-SEW SIDE PANELS

For a no-sew window treatment with a light, unstructured appearance, drape soft, lightweight fabric panels over swinging extenders, or crane rods, to create a deep valance and elegant floor puddles. This treatment is suitable for full coverage on narrow windows or as side panels on wider windows.

Swinging extender rods are mounted to a bracket on one end and can swing out to expose the window view. The rods pictured were purchased at an antique shop. Decorative and utility crane rods are available from specialty window hardware suppliers or through decorators.

Choose a soft, lightweight fabric that appears the same from both sides and has an attractive or minimal selvage. If the fabric ravels, you may want to finish the lower edge of the drapery panel.

CUTTING DIRECTIONS

Measure from the top of the installed rod to the floor. Use one width of fabric for each panel, with the length of each panel equal to the measured distance plus 60" (152.5 cm) to allow for the valance and floor puddle.

HOW TO MAKE DRAPED SIDE PANELS

MATERIALS

- Lightweight fabric, at least 54" (137 cm) wide.
- Swinging extender rod set.
- Double-stick carpet tape.

1 Cut and apply double-stick tape to back side of rod. Drape the upper edge of fabric over rod, with about 4" (10 cm) folded to back side; secure fabric to tape, distributing fullness evenly.

2 Gather the fabric loosely about 36" (91.5 cm) below the rod, using hands; fold bottom of panel up and over rod, with hand gathers at top of rod, forming 18" (46 cm) valance.

3 Arrange the valance, distributing the fullness evenly and folding in the selvages.

4 Arrange bottom of panel on floor, draping it loosely and concealing the raw edges and selvages of the fabric.

EASY-TO-SEW
CURTAIN PANELS

With an emphasis on decorative hardware, the window treatments can simply be panels of fabric. These versatile panels have a relaxed look, curving or swooping across the top and puddling onto the floor. Hang the panels from a decorative pole, using rings. Or attach grommets along the top of the panel, to accommodate decorative hooks or even the rod itself.

As shown here and on page 63, the amount of fullness can affect the look of the curtain panels. The amount of drape along the top of the panels can be varied by the number of rings or grommets used as well as by the spacing between them.

When designing curtain panels for rooms needing little light control or privacy, consider unlined curtains and sheers as well as side panels that leave most or all of the window glass exposed. You may prefer to line the curtain panels, to add body and prevent the decorator fabric from fading.

Large grommets (opposite), attached below the hem at the top of a lined curtain panel, are speared by a decorative arrow-style rod. For gentle, rolling curves, two times fullness is used. Large grommets may be purchased and installed at a tent and awning store.

Curtain panels (inset, opposite) are hung from rings on a thin decorator rod. For dramatic draping, three times fullness is used, and the fabric swoops between the widely spaced rings.

Grommets (right), centered on the top hem of the curtain panel, are hooked onto a decorative pole. For a simple, controlled look, only one and one-half times fullness is used.

MATERIALS

- Decorator fabric in weight suitable for desired style.
- Lining fabric, optional.
- Decorator rod.
- Hardware items as needed, including grommets and decorative hooks or clip-on or sew-on rings.

CUTTING DIRECTONS

Determine the desired finished length of the panels. To determine the cut length, add 4" (10 cm) for 1" (2.5 cm) double-fold hems at the upper and lower edges and 18" to 24" (46 to 61 cm) for puddling on the floor.

Decide on the desired fullness of the panels (opposite). Multiply the desired finished length of the rod times the desired fullness; divide this amount by the width of the fabric to determine the number of fabric widths required. Use full or half widths of fabric.

HOW TO SEW A CURTAIN PANEL

1 **Unlined panel**. Seam the fabric widths, if more than one width is desired for the panel. Press under 1" (2.5 cm) twice at the lower edge of panel; stitch double-fold hem. Repeat for a 1" (2.5 cm) double-fold hem at upper edge, then at sides.

2 Plan and pin-mark the spacing for rings or grommets at top of the curtain panel. As shown opposite, if fewer rings or grommets are used, spaced farther apart, more fabric drapes between them. For a more controlled look, use more rings or grommets, spaced closer together.

3 Check the drape of the panel by securing it at pin marks to the side of an ironing board, with markings spaced the desired distance apart. Adjust number of rings or grommets and the spacing between them, if necessary. Use an even number of grommets if rod will be inserted through them.

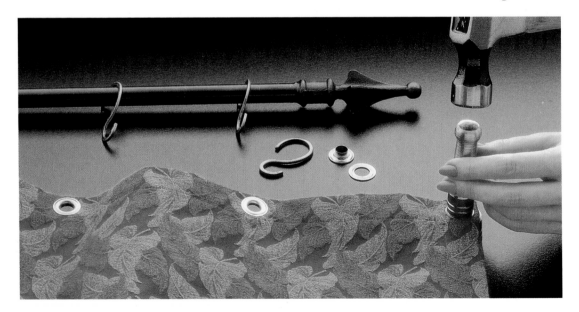

4 Attach the grommets to top of panel at the markings, following the manufacturer's directions; insert hooks into the grommets. Or attach sew-on or clip-on rings. Hang panels from decorative rod.

5 Arrange the fabric to puddle onto the floor, if desired.

Lined panel. Seam the fabric widths, if more than one is desired for panel. Place the lining and decorator fabric wrong sides together, matching the raw edges. Press and stitch 1" (2.5 cm) double-fold hems as in step 1, opposite, folding both fabrics together as one. Finish as in steps 2 to 5.

ACHIEVING DIFFERENT LOOKS WITH FABRIC FULLNESS & THE SPACING OF THE HARDWARE

Different fabric fullnesses and same spacing between hooks. For a flatter panel, one-and-one-half times fullness is used (left); this means, the width of the curtain measures one-and-one-half times the length of the rod. For a fuller panel use two times fullness (middle) or two-and-one-half times fullness (right). All hooks are spaced 15½" (39.3 cm) apart.

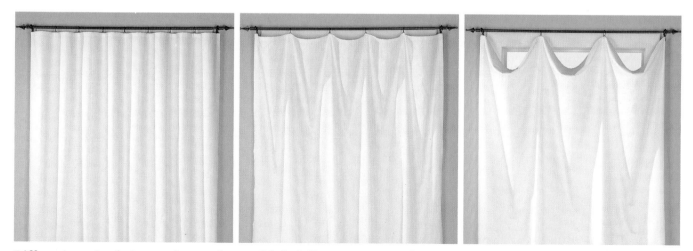

Different spacing between rings and same fabric fullness. For a controlled look along the top of the curtain, use more rings and space them close together (left). For a softer look, use fewer rings with more space between them (middle). For dramatic swoops in the fabric, use a minimum of rings, spaced even farther apart (right). All curtain panels have two times fullness.

FABRIC PANELS WITH LACING

Lacing fabric panels over a pole set or decorative rod is another variation of the easy-to-sew curtain panel (page 61). Space the grommets or rings for a loose, unstructured drape (page 63) and use cording, ribbon, or leather lacing threaded through the grommets or rings.

Select a soft, lightweight fabric for the best draping results. If the fabric is sheer, reinforce it with nylon net where the grommets or rings are attached.

For a conventional drape, the end grommets or rings are positioned at the outer corners of the panels; this method must be used if you will be opening and closing the panels or if the rod has a return. To accentuate the unstructured look with draped corners, the end grommets or rings are placed 5" to 8" (12.5 to 20.5 cm) from the corners.

CUTTING DIRECTIONS

Determine the finished panel length by measuring from the bottom of the pole or rod to where you want the lower edge of the curtain; then subtract the space you want between the bottom of the pole and the upper edge of the panel. For floor-length panels, allow ½" (1.3 cm) clearance between the drapery and the floor. For floor puddles, add 18" to 24" (46 to 61 cm).

The cut length of the fabric is equal to the desired finished length of the panel plus 3" (7.5 cm) for the top hem. Also add 8" (20.5 cm) for a double 4" (10 cm) hem at the lower edge; if the panel will be floor-puddled, add only 2" (5 cm) for a double 1" (2.5 cm) hem.

The total cut width of the decorator fabric is equal to two-and-one-half times the length of the pole or rod. Divide this total in half for two panels, and for each panel add 6" (15 cm) for side hems. If it is necessary to piece fabric widths together, also add 1" (2.5 cm) for each seam.

Determine the spacing and number of grommets for each curtain panel. The grommets are spaced 10" to 15" (25.5 to 38 cm) apart, depending upon the amount of drape desired between grommets. For draped corners, position the end grommets in from the outer corners a distance equal to one-half the width of the spacing between grommets.

HOW TO MAKE GROMMET PANELS WITH LACING

MATERIALS

- Lightweight decorator fabric.
- Pole set or decorative curtain rod.
- Size 0, or ¼" (6 mm), grommets; attaching tool.
- Lacing.
- Nylon netting, for reinforcing sheer fabric.

1 Seam fabric widths together for each panel, using ½" (1.3 cm) seam allowance; finish seams. At lower edge of panel, press under 4" (10 cm) twice to wrong side for floor-length panels; press under 1" (2.5 cm) twice for floor-puddled panels. Stitch to make double-fold hem, using straight stitch or blindstitch. (Contrasting thread was used to show detail.)

2 Press under 1½" (3.8 cm) twice on sides. Stitch to make double-fold hems, using straight stitch or blindstitch.

3 Press under 1½" (3.8 cm) twice at upper edge to make double-fold hem. Trim out the excess layers of fabric at corners.

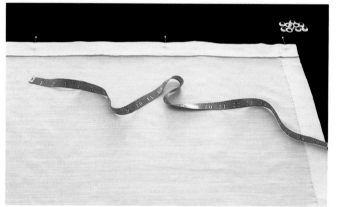

4 Mark the spacing for grommets, placing marks at ends for conventional drape or in from the side edges a distance equal to one-half the width of the spacing for draped corners. Space the remaining grommets evenly between the end markings.

5 Reinforce sheer decorator fabric by positioning a 1½" (3.8 cm) square of net in first fold of upper hem at each grommet marking. Fold and stitch hem, using straight stitch or blindstitch.

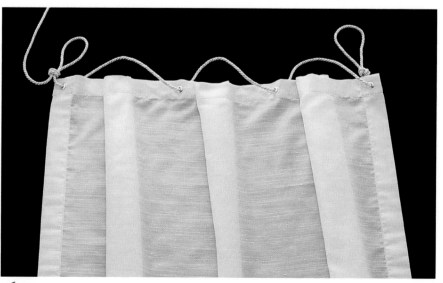

6 Fasten grommets securely, using fastening tool (page 62); position upper edge of grommets about ½" (1.3 cm) from upper edge of panel. Insert lacing strips through grommets, and tie knots or bows around pole or rod. Install pole.

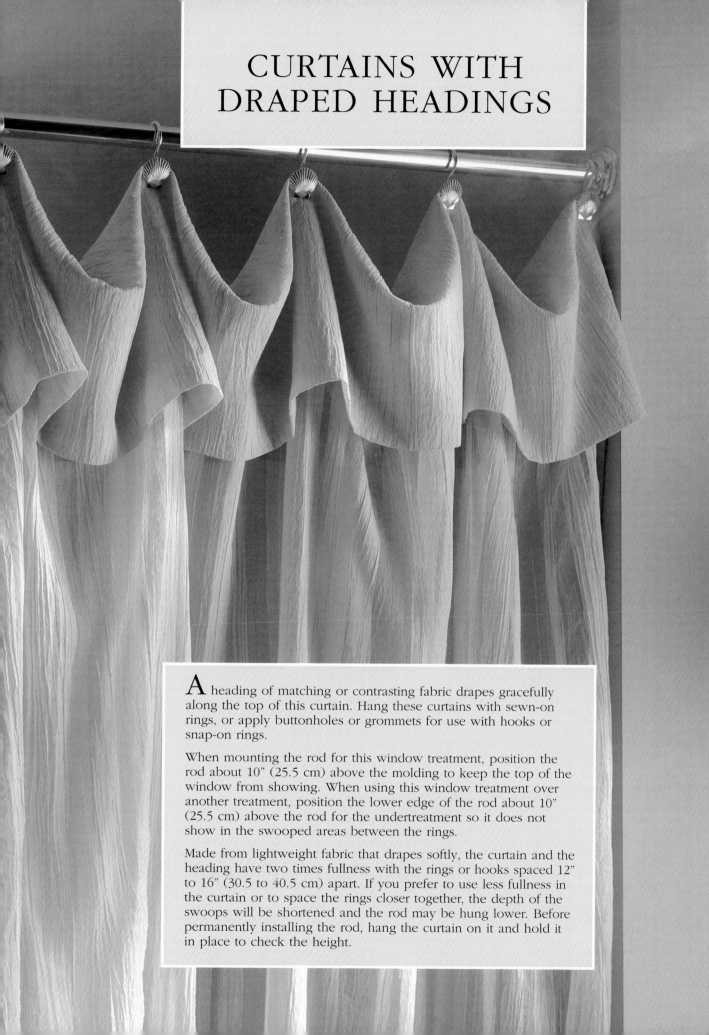

CURTAINS WITH DRAPED HEADINGS

A heading of matching or contrasting fabric drapes gracefully along the top of this curtain. Hang these curtains with sewn-on rings, or apply buttonholes or grommets for use with hooks or snap-on rings.

When mounting the rod for this window treatment, position the rod about 10" (25.5 cm) above the molding to keep the top of the window from showing. When using this window treatment over another treatment, position the lower edge of the rod about 10" (25.5 cm) above the rod for the undertreatment so it does not show in the swooped areas between the rings.

Made from lightweight fabric that drapes softly, the curtain and the heading have two times fullness with the rings or hooks spaced 12" to 16" (30.5 to 40.5 cm) apart. If you prefer to use less fullness in the curtain or to space the rings closer together, the depth of the swoops will be shortened and the rod may be hung lower. Before permanently installing the rod, hang the curtain on it and hold it in place to check the height.

HOW TO SEW A CURTAIN WITH A DRAPED HEADING

MATERIALS

• Lightweight fabric that drapes softly, for the curtain; matching or contrasting lightweight, soft fabric may be used for the heading.

• Grommets and attaching tool, optional.

• Wooden pole with sew-on wooden rings, or curtain rod with hooks or snap-on rings.

CUTTING DIRECTIONS

Determine the approximate height for mounting the curtain rod (page 67), about 10" (25.5 cm) above the window frame.

Determine the desired finished length of the curtain by first measuring from the bottom of the rod to the floor. Subtract 2½" (6.5 cm) from this measurement, because, when hung, the curtain is about 2½" (6.5 cm) below the rod. Then subtract an amount equal to the desired clearance from the floor, usually about ½" (1.3 cm).

The cut length of the fabric is equal to the desired finished length of the curtain plus 5½" (14 cm). The cut width of the fabric is equal to two times the length of the rod plus 4" (10 cm); this allows for two 1" (2.5 cm) double-fold side hems. Seam the fabric widths together as necessary; if desired, stitch French seams as on page 20.

For the heading, cut matching or contrasting fabric into 29" (73.5 cm) lengths. Seam the fabric widths together as necessary so the heading is equal to the hemmed width of the curtain plus 1" (2.5 cm) for seam allowances on the sides.

1 Seam fabric widths together. Press under 4" (10 cm) twice on lower edge of curtain panel; stitch to make 4" (10 cm) double-fold hem. Press under 1" (2.5 cm) twice on each side of curtain panel; stitch to make 1" (2.5 cm) double-fold side hems.

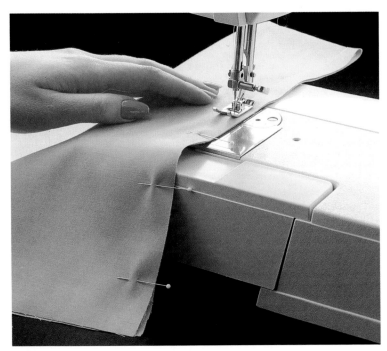

2 Seam fabric widths together for heading, using ½" (1.3 cm) conventional seams; French seams are not used. Press seams open. Fold heading in half lengthwise, right sides together; at ends, stitch ½" (1.3 cm) seams.

3 Turn the heading right side out; press the seams at ends. Baste the raw edges together; press along the fold.

4 Pin the heading to the top of the curtain panel, matching raw edges, with the right side of the heading facing down on the wrong side of the curtain panel. Stitch ½" (1.3 cm) seam; finish the seam, using zigzag or overlock stitch.

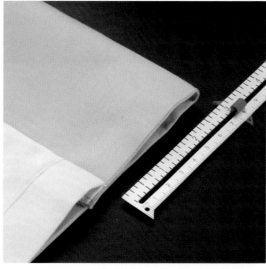

5 Fold the heading 3" (7.5 cm) above seamline as shown. Pin in place; do not press foldline.

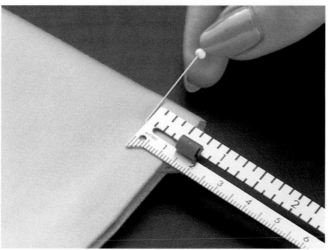

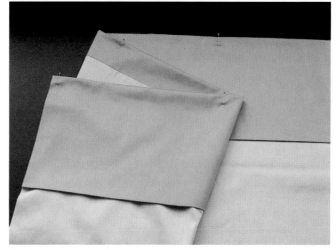

6 Mark fold at upper edge, ½" (1.3 cm) from each side of the curtain panel, to mark placement for end rings.

7 Mark placement for remaining rings, about 12" to 16" (30.5 to 40.5 cm) apart, dividing the distance between end marks evenly.

8 Sew rings to back side of heading at markings, using small stitches around entire metal eye **(a).** Or stitch buttonholes **(b)** or attach grommets **(c),** with the top of each buttonhole or grommet ½" (1.3 cm) below the fold at the upper edge; stitch buttonholes or attach grommets through all four layers of heading and curtain panel.

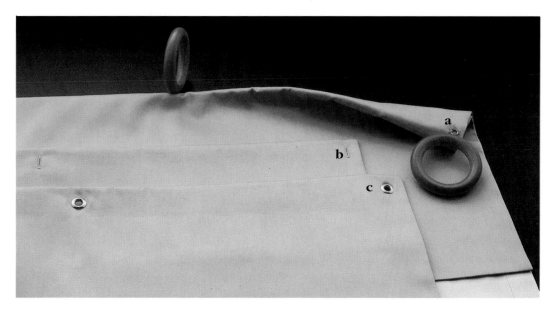

TAB CURTAINS

Tab curtains are unlined panels with long or short tabs and a facing at the upper edge. The facing may be cut from contrasting fabric and folded to the front of the panel for a banded effect. The facing strip should have a finished width of 1" (2.5 cm) or wider if a contrasting band is desired.

Hang the curtains from a decorative pole set mounted on or above the window frame. Or, for a unique look, hang them from decorative knobs (page 54) mounted 4" to 10" (10 to 25.5 cm) apart.

CUTTING DIRECTIONS

Determine the desired finished length of the curtain by measuring from the bottom of the pole or knob to the desired finished hem; then subtract the distance desired between the lower edge of the pole or knob and the upper edge of the curtain.

The cut length of the curtain is equal to the desired finished length of the curtain plus 2½" (6.5 cm) for hem and seam allowance.

The cut width of the curtain is equal to one-and-one-half to two times the length of the pole or width of the window. If you are sewing two curtain panels, divide this measurement by two to determine the cut width of each panel. For each panel, add 4" (10 cm) for side hems. If it is necessary to piece fabric widths together to make the panel, also add 1" (2.5 cm) for each seam.

Determine the spacing and the number of tabs for each curtain panel; tabs are spaced 6" to 12" (15 to 30.5 cm) apart, depending on the amount of fullness desired between the tabs. Cut two strips of fabric for each tab, 1¼" (3.2 cm) × 5" to 9" (12.5 to 23 cm).

Cut the facing strip twice the desired width plus 1" (2.5 cm) for seam allowances. The cut length of the strip equals the cut width of the panel; piece as necessary.

Tab curtains can be designed for a variety of looks. The tab curtains above have a coordinating band at the upper edge and are mounted on a pole set. The tab curtain opposite hangs from decorative knobs and is pulled to the side with a length of cording.

HOW TO SEW TAB CURTAINS

1 Stitch fabric widths together for each panel, stitching ½" (1.3 cm) seams. Finish the seams. At lower edge of the panel, press under 1" (2.5 cm) twice to wrong side of panel; stitch, using straight stitch or blindstitch, to make double-fold hem.

2 Place two tab strips right sides together, matching raw edges. Stitch ¼" (6 mm) seam on long edges. Repeat for remaining tabs. Turn tabs right side out, and press.

3 Fold tabs in half. Pin to upper edge of curtain panel, matching raw edges. Pin tabs to right side of panel if facing will be folded to wrong side; pin tabs to wrong side of panel if facing will be folded to the right side for contrasting band. Place tabs at ends 2" (5 cm) from each side; space remaining tabs evenly between the end tabs. Machine-baste tabs in place.

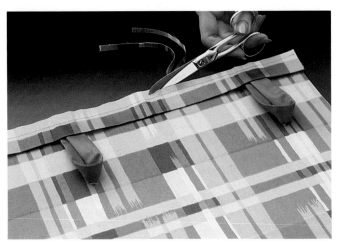

4 Fold the facing strip in half lengthwise, wrong sides together; press. Pin the facing to right side of panel at upper edge, matching raw edges; or, for contrasting band, pin to wrong side of panel. Stitch ½" (1.3 cm) seam at upper edge; trim to ¼" (6 mm).

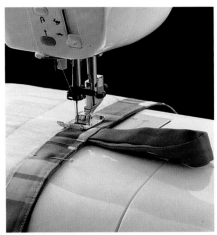

5 Press the facing to wrong side of panel; or, for contrasting band, press the band to right side. Topstitch close to upper edge and folded edge of facing or band.

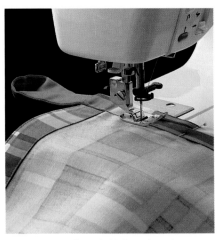

6 Press under 1" (2.5 cm) twice at the sides. Stitch to make double-fold hems, using a straight stitch or blindstitch.

7 Hang the curtain panel from knobs or from a decorative pole set.

TENT-FLAP CURTAINS

Tent-flap curtains add an uncluttered, stylish look to windows. Depending on the fabric choice and the draping of the flaps, tent-flap curtains can be tailored or unstructured in style. These curtains work especially well on small windows.

The folded flaps of the curtains can be hand-tacked in place, or they can be secured with a button and buttonhole to allow for opening and closing. The style of the folded flaps may vary with the size of the window. Experiment by folding back the front edges and corners of the panels to determine the most suitable style for a particular window.

Tent-flap curtains are attached to a mounting board and may be mounted either inside or outside the window frame. For an inside mount, use a 1 × 1 mounting board. Cut the mounting board ½" (1.3 cm) shorter than the inside measurement of the window frame; this ensures that the mounting board will fit inside the frame after it is covered with fabric. For an outside mount, use a 1 × 2 mounting board. An outside-mounted board may be mounted either at the top of the window frame or on the wall above the window. Cut the mounting board at least 2" (5 cm) longer than the window frame to allow space for mounting the angle irons. Secure the angle irons to wall studs whenever possible, using pan-head screws. Or use molly bolts if the angle irons do not align with the wall studs.

MATERIALS

- Decorator fabric, for curtains and covered mounting board.
- Matching or contrasting fabric, for lining.
- Mounting board.
- Heavy-duty stapler; staples.
- Angle irons and 8 × ¾" (2 cm) pan-head screws or molly bolts, for outside mount.
- Two 1½" (3.8 cm) lengths of 1 × 2 board and self-adhesive hook and loop tape, for outside mount.
- 8 × 1½" (3.8 cm) pan-head screws, for inside mount.
- Two cup hooks and two small rings, for inside mount.

CUTTING DIRECTIONS

The cut length of each curtain panel is equal to the desired finished length plus the depth of the mounting board plus 1" (2.5 cm) for ½" (1.3 cm) seam allowances. The cut width of each panel is equal to one-half the width of the mounting board plus 2" (5 cm) to allow for seam allowances and 1" (2.5 cm) overlap. For outside-mounted curtains, also add the depth, or projection, of the mounting board. Cut two panels each, from fabric and lining, to this length and width.

Tent-flap curtains may be mounted inside or outside the window frame. Above, inside-mounted curtains are constructed from two sheer fabrics. On page 74, outside-mounted curtains made from decorator fabric have a contrasting lining fabric for a coordinated look.

HOW TO SEW OUTSIDE-MOUNTED TENT-FLAP CURTAINS

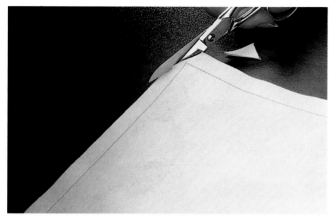

1 Cover mounting board (page 16). Set aside until step 4. Pin outer panel fabric to lining, right sides together, matching raw edges. Stitch ½" (1.3 cm) seams on all sides; leave 8" (20.5 cm) opening at center of upper edge for turning. Trim corners.

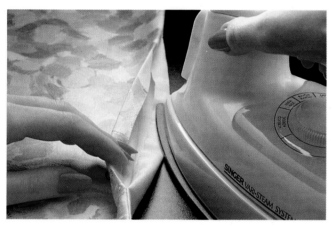

2 Press seam allowances open. Trim seams, if necessary. Turn panel right side out. Press edges, pressing in seam allowances at center opening.

3 Stitch horizontal buttonhole at the inside edge of each panel or diagonal buttonholes at the lower inside corner, if desired.

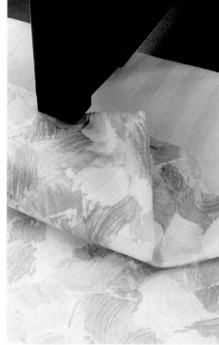

4 Staple panels to the board, aligning upper edge of panels to back edge of board; at corner, make diagonal fold to form a miter. Panels will overlap 1" (2.5 cm) at the center.

5 Install outside-mounted board as on page 17, steps 1 to 5.

(Continued)

6 Fold the corner or front edge of each panel back to the outer edges as desired; pin in place, making sure sides are even. Attach button to use with buttonhole, or hand-tack the layers together and embellish with decorative button.

7 Cut 1½" (3.8 cm) length from excess mounting board for the projection on each side of window. Mount one block of wood on each side of window frame, at about the height of button placement, using angle irons. Secure the lining to wood with small piece of self-adhesive hook and loop tape.

HOW TO SEW INSIDE-MOUNTED TENT-FLAP CURTAINS

1 Follow steps 1 to 3 on page 75; staple panels on mounting board, overlapping them 1" (2.5 cm) so they are centered on board. Panels may extend slightly beyond the ends of the board.

2 Mount curtain by securing board inside of window frame, using 8 × 1½" (3.8 cm) pan-head screws; predrill the holes, using ⅛" drill bit.

3 Stitch small ring to curtain lining at lower outside edge. Position a cup hook inside frame, and secure. Attach ring to hook. Complete the curtains as in step 6, above.

Draped tent-flap curtains *have a relaxed look. The soft draping is achieved by fastening the corners of the panels near the top of the curtain. Buttons and fabric button loops are used to fasten the flaps.*

Lace and sheer fabric *make tent-flap curtains that filter sunlight. Ribbon bows are tacked to the front of the flaps for embellishment.*

Single flap *is secured to the front of an inside-mounted board, using buttons and buttonholes. Buttons are stitched to the fabric-covered mounting board, and buttonholes are stitched at the upper edge of the fabric panel.*

Creative Rod-pocket Curtains

ROD-POCKET BASICS

Rod-pocket curtains are often the choice when selecting a stationary window treatment that is stylish and easy to sew. Many different looks can be achieved with rod-pocket curtains, including interesting variations for headings (pages 104 and 105) and ruffles (page 90).

Several types of rods may be used for rod-pocket curtains, including flat rods in widths of 1", 2½", and 4½" (2.5, 6.5, and 11.5 cm). Wood and metal pole sets, used with elbows or finials, may also be used and are available in several diameters. Poles can also be created, using PVC pipe and fittings as on page 13.

When a pole set with elbows is used, the outer edges of the curtain panels wrap around the elbows to the wall. For curtains mounted on poles with finials, returns can be created by making an opening in the front of the rod-pocket for inserting the pole.

Unlined rod-pocket curtains can be made from sheers or laces, creating a lightweight treatment that allows filtered light to enter the room. For curtains made from mediumweight to heavyweight decorator fabrics, lining is used to make the curtains more durable, add extra body, and support the side hems and headings.

Before cutting the fabric, decide where the window treatment should be positioned and install the curtain rod or pole. Measure from the lower edge of the rod to where you want the lower edge of the curtain. To determine the finished length of the curtain, add the desired depth of the heading and rod pocket to this measurement. This is the finished length of the curtain panel from the top of the heading to the hemmed lower edge.

MATERIALS

- Decorator fabric.
- Lining fabric, optional.
- Drapery weights.
- Curtain rod or pole set with finials or elbows.
- Wooden brackets, keyhole brackets, or elbow brackets, for mounting pole.

TERMS TO KNOW

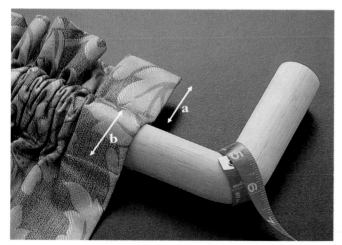

Heading (a) is the portion at the top of a rod-pocket curtain that forms a ruffle when the curtain is on the rod. The depth of the heading is the distance from the top of the finished curtain to the top stitching line of the rod pocket.

Rod pocket (b) is the portion of the curtain where the curtain rod or pole is inserted; stitching lines at the top and bottom of the rod pocket keep the rod in place. To determine the depth of the rod pocket, measure around the widest part of the rod or pole; add ½" (1.3 cm) ease to this measurement, and divide by two.

Returns can be created for rod-pocket curtains that are mounted on poles with finials. The pole is inserted through an opening in the front of the rod pocket, allowing the side of the curtain to return to the wall.

Determine the depth of the rod pocket and heading (page 81) and the depth of the hem at the lower edge. A 4" (10 cm) double-fold hem is often used for the decorator fabric; if the curtain is lined, a 2" (5 cm) double-fold hem is used for the lining.

The cut length of the decorator fabric is equal to the desired finished length of the curtain plus the depth of the heading and the rod pocket plus ½" (1.3 cm) for turn-under at the upper edge plus twice the depth of the hem.

The cut width of the decorator fabric is determined by the length of the curtain rod, including the returns, multiplied by the amount of fullness desired in the curtain.

For sheer fabrics, allow two-and-one-half to three times the length of the rod for fullness; for heavier fabrics, allow two to two-and-one-half times. After multiplying the length of the rod times the desired fullness, divide this number by the number of panels being used for the treatment; add 6" (15 cm) for each panel to allow for 1½" (3.8 cm) double-fold side hems. If it is necessary to piece fabric widths together to make each panel, also add 1" (2.5 cm) for each seam.

Cut the lining fabric 5" (12.5 cm) shorter than the decorator fabric; the cut width of the lining is the same as the decorator fabric.

HOW TO SEW UNLINED ROD-POCKET CURTAINS

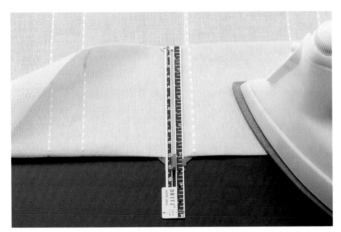

1 Seam fabric widths, if necessary, for each curtain panel. At lower edge, press under an amount equal to the hem depth; repeat to press under a double-fold hem. Stitch, using straight stitch or blindstitch.

2 Press under 1½" (3.8 cm) twice on sides. Tack drapery weights inside the side hems, about 3" (7.5 cm) from lower edge. Stitch to make double-fold hems.

3 Press under ½" (1.3 cm) on upper edge. Then press under an amount equal to rod-pocket depth plus heading depth. If curtains will be mounted on pole with elbow returns, omit steps 4 to 6.

4 Mount rod on wooden, keyhole, or elbow bracket. Measure distance from the wall to center of the pole, as indicated by arrow.

5 Unfold upper edge of curtain on return side of panel. On right side of fabric, measure from the hemmed side edge of curtain a distance equal to the measurement in step 4; mark at center of rod pocket. If curtains will be mounted on rod with key-hole brackets, omit step 6.

6 Cut 1" (2.5 cm) strip of fusible interfacing, 1" (2.5 cm) longer than depth of the rod pocket, if the curtains will be mounted on a pole with wooden brackets. Fuse strip to wrong side of curtain panel, centering it directly under mark in step 5. On right side of panel, stitch a buttonhole at the mark, from top to bottom of rod pocket. Refold upper edge of panel along pressed lines; pin.

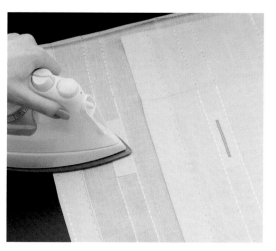

7 Stitch close to first fold; stitch again at depth of heading, using tape on bed of sewing machine as stitching guide.

HOW TO SEW LINED ROD-POCKET CURTAINS

1 Follow step 1, opposite. Repeat for the lining, pressing under and stitching a 2" (5 cm) double-fold hem in the lining.

2 Place curtain panel and lining panel wrong sides together, matching the raw edges at the sides and upper edge; pin. At the bottom, the lining panel will be 1" (2.5 cm) shorter than curtain panel. Complete the curtain as on page 82, steps 2 through 7, handling decorator fabric and lining as one fabric.

HOW TO INSTALL ROD-POCKET CURTAINS

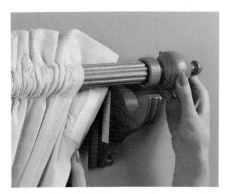

Pole with wooden brackets and finials. Remove the finials; insert pole into rod pocket with ends of the pole extending through the buttonholes. Reattach finials; mount pole. Secure return to the wooden bracket, using self-adhesive hook and loop tape.

Pole with keyhole bracket and finials. Slit center of the rod pocket at point marked in step 5, opposite. Insert pole into rod pocket. Pull return over end of pole, aligning slit to finial screw hole; attach finials through slits, and mount pole. Attach a pin-on ring to inner edge of return, and secure to a tenter hook or cup hook in wall.

Pole with elbows. Insert the pole through the rod pocket; pull the curtain back to expose small screws. Mount the pole on brackets. Slide the curtain over brackets.

TUCKED & BISHOP-SLEEVE CURTAINS

Tucked curtains *(opposite) feature tucks near the lower edge. A deeper 8" (20.5 cm) double-fold hem creates a smooth visual flow below the lowest tuck in this style, which is often made with sheer fabrics.*

Bishop-sleeve curtains *(page 86) are elegantly pouffed and allowed to puddle lavishly on the floor. The curtain and valance are hung on separate rods.*

HOW TO MAKE TUCKED CURTAINS

MATERIALS

- Lightweight or sheer decorator fabric.
- Curtain rod.

CUTTING DIRECTIONS

Cut rod-pocket curtain panels as on page 82, allowing 16" (40.5 cm) for an 8" (20.5 cm) double-fold hem at the lower edge; add 9" (23 cm) of length for three tucks.

1 Seam fabric widths, if necessary, for each curtain panel. At lower edge, press under 8" (20.5 cm) twice to wrong side; stitch to make double-fold hem. With wrong sides of fabric together, press foldline for tuck 1⅝" (4 cm) from upper edge of hem.

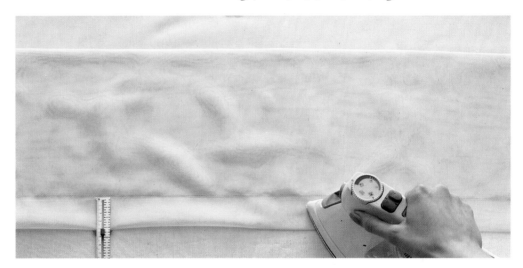

2 Press second foldline 6" (15 cm) away from first foldline; press third foldline 6" (15 cm) away from second foldline.

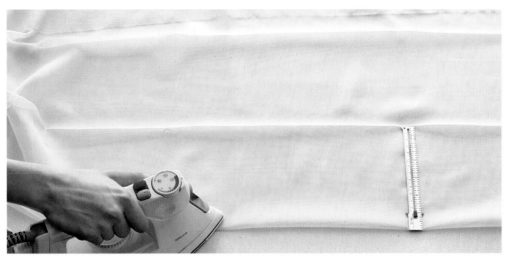

3 Stitch the tucks 1½" (3.8 cm) from foldlines. For easier stitching, place tape on bed of sewing machine to use as a guide. Press tucks toward lower edge. Complete curtain, following steps 2 to 7 on pages 82 and 83.

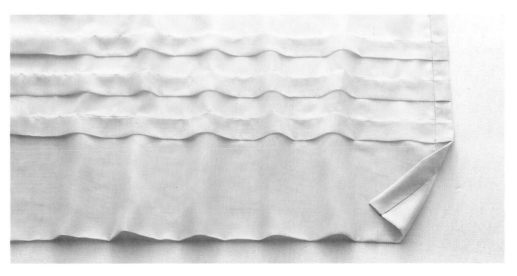

HOW TO MAKE BISHOP-SLEEVE CURTAINS

MATERIALS

- Decorator fabric.
- Curtain rod; tenter hooks or cup hooks.
- Cording; bodkin or safety pin.
- Tissue paper, optional.

CUTTING DIRECTIONS

Cut two curtain panels, using one fabric width for each panel. Calculate the cut length of each panel as for rod-pocket curtains on page 82, allowing 2" (5 cm) for a 1" (2.5 cm) double-fold hem at the lower edge; add an extra 12" (30.5 cm) of length for each pouf and 12" (30.5 cm) to puddle on the floor.

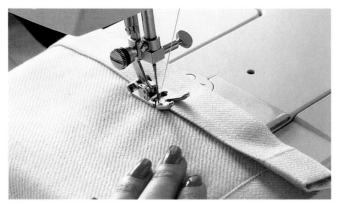

1 Press under and stitch 1½" (3.8 cm) side hems. Press under and stitch 1" (2.5 cm) lower hem. Stitch rod pocket and heading (pages 82 and 83, steps 3 to 7).

2 Insert a cord into hem at lower edge, using bodkin or safety pin. Pull cord tightly to gather lower edge.

3 Insert curtain rod through rod pockets, gathering fabric evenly. Install rod on brackets. Determine location of poufs by tightly bunching panel with hands and lifting it to desired position.

4 Attach tenter hook or cup hook behind each pouf to hold tieback. Secure tieback tightly. Tuck tissue paper into pouf, if desired, to improve blousing.

5 Arrange bottom of bishop-sleeve curtain, puddling fabric onto floor.

DECORATING WITH OLD LINENS

The beautiful bed, kitchen, and table linens from years past proudly display various types of needlework, from embroidery to cutwork to handmade laces. Whether you own cherished heirlooms handed down in the family or just-found treasures from an antique store, these linens can add a special touch to your home decorating. An item that is stained may be arranged so the stains are concealed while it is on display. Or you can salvage the undamaged portions of the item to use for making pillows or other small accessories.

Unmatched tablecloths *in assorted prints are made into curtains, with clusters of artificial grapes used as tiebacks.*

Make a rod pocket at the top of the curtain panel, folding down the upper edge of the tablecloth **(a).** Or, if the tablecloth is too short to fold down the top, add a strip of fabric for the rod pocket **(b)** or for a facing at the upper edge **(c).**

CURTAINS FROM SHEETS

Create curtains quickly, using decorative sheets with embellished edges. For a romantic window treatment, choose ruffled sheets or sheets with lace trims. For a more tailored look, select sheets with flat or pleated borders. And for imaginative valances, use pillow shams that coordinate.

The decorative edge of the sheet may be used at the inner, upper, or lower edge of a curtain panel, depending on the style of the window treatment. Decide where you want to position the decorative edge and how much fullness you want the curtain to have. Then determine the sheet size you will need, allowing for any headings, rod pockets, and hems.

For best results, purchase good-quality sheets with a high thread count. When selecting patterned sheets, keep in mind that some one-way designs may not be suitable if the sheet will be turned sideways or upside down. If the ruffle or border will be used vertically on the curtain, the width of the sheet must be long enough for the cut length of the curtain.

Cutwork borders become the decorative lower edges of rod-pocket curtains and valance.

Sheets with printed borders create curtains with a tailored look. So the border can be used as the heading of the curtain, a separate piece of fabric is stitched on the wrong side of the sheet for the rod pocket.

Pillow sham (opposite) makes a coordinated top treatment for curtains from sheets. Fold the sham diagonally and secure it to a decorative wood pole, using double-stick tape.

RUFFLED CURTAINS

Double ruffle *(above) is featured on these tieback curtains, along with ruffled tiebacks (page 115). The ruffles extend only to the bottom of the rod pocket, which allows the shirred fabric to continue uninterrupted across the top of the curtains.*

Single ruffle *(left) in a contrasting fabric trims this single-panel curtain. The ruffle extends to the top of the heading.*

Ruffled curtains add coziness and charm to a room, blending well into various decorating schemes. Deep ruffles on full curtains are romantic and frilly, while narrow ruffles that define the edge of a damask panel are elegant. For a uniform look, make the ruffle from the same fabric as the curtain. Or use a contrasting fabric for the ruffle, perhaps repeating the fabric on ruffled tiebacks (page 115).

Choose from either single or double ruffles. In the method for double ruffles, bulk is eliminated at the seamline, for easier sewing and softer gathers. With both styles, the ruffles are self-faced and sewn into the seam between the curtain fabric and the lining. They are applied to the inner and lower edges of the curtain, curving around the rounded corners of the curtain panels.

For two panels that meet in the center and tie back, begin the ruffle just under the rod pocket on each panel, allowing for an uninterrupted heading across the curtain rod. For separated side panels or a single panel tied to one side, begin the ruffle at the top of the heading.

MATERIALS

- Decorator fabric, for curtain panels.
- Matching or contrasting fabric, for the ruffle.
- Lining fabric.
- Drapery weights.
- Curtain rod.

HOW TO MAKE ROD-POCKET CURTAINS WITH A SINGLE RUFFLE

CUTTING DIRECTIONS

Determine the desired finished length of the curtain, from the top of the heading to the lower edge of the ruffle. Cut the decorator fabric for each curtain panel with the cut length equal to the desired finished length of the curtain minus the finished width of the ruffle, plus the depth of the heading and rod pocket, plus 1" (2.5 cm) for seam allowance and turn-under.

Determine the cut width of each curtain panel by multiplying the length of the rod times the desired fullness (page 19); divide this number by the number of panels being used for the treatment, and add 3½" (9 cm) for each panel to allow for a 1½" (3.8 cm) double-fold

hem on the return side of the panel plus ½" (1.3 cm) for the seam on the ruffled side. If it is necessary to piece fabric widths together to make each panel, also add 1" (2.5 cm) for each seam.

Cut the lining for each panel to the same length and width as the decorator fabric.

For the ruffles, cut fabric strips on the crosswise grain, with the width of the strips equal to twice the desired finished width of the ruffle plus 1" (2.5 cm). Cut as many strips as necessary for a combined length of two to two-and-one-half times the length to be ruffled.

1 Stitch the fabric strips for the ruffle together in ¼" (6 mm) seams, right sides together. Press seams open. Fold ends of strips in half lengthwise, right sides together; stitch across the ends in ¼" (6 mm) seams. Turn right side out, and fold strip in half lengthwise, matching raw edges; press foldline and ends of ruffle strip.

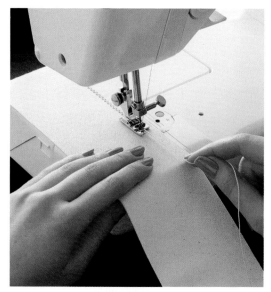

2 Zigzag over a cord on back side of ruffle strip within ½" (1.3 cm) seam allowance, stitching through both layers of ruffle strip.

(Continued)

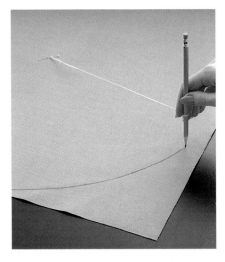

3 Seam the fabric widths and lining widths, if necessary, for each panel. Curve inside lower edge of one curtain panel by drawing an arc with pencil and string from a pivot point 12" (30.5 cm) up from the bottom and in from the side.

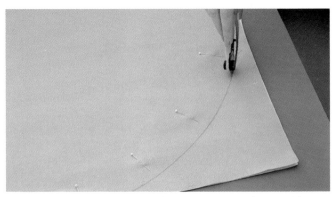

4 Place curtain panel over lining, wrong sides together, matching edges; cut curve along marked line through curtain panel and lining. Repeat for the second panel and lining, if any, curving opposite corner.

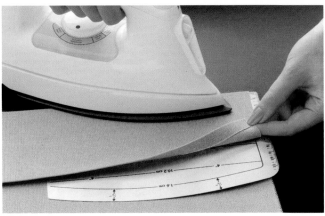

5 Press under ½" (1.3 cm) on the upper edge of curtain panel. Then press under an amount equal to the rod-pocket depth plus heading depth. If you are making a curtain panel with ruffle beginning below the rod pocket, pin-mark location of lower stitching line for rod pocket; unfold pressed edge.

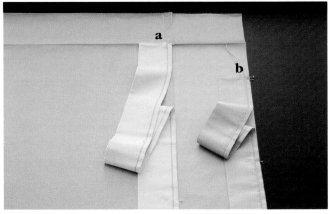

6 Divide ruffle strip into eighths; pin-mark. Divide edges of curtain panel to be ruffled into eighths, beginning at top of heading **(a)** or at lower stitching line of rod pocket **(b)** and ending on lower edge 3" (7.5 cm) from raw edge on return side of panel. Pin ruffle strip to right side of the curtain panel, matching pin marks and raw edges.

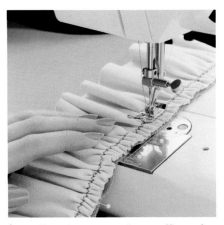

7 Pull gathering cord on ruffle to fit edge of the curtain panel; pin in place. Stitch a scant ½" (1.3 cm) from the raw edges.

8 Pin lining to curtain panel, right sides together, matching the raw edges on ruffled side of panel; stitch ½" (1.3 cm) seam on ruffled side.

9 Turn right side out, matching remaining raw edges of curtain panel and lining. Press seam.

10 Press under 1½" (3.8 cm) twice on unruffled side of the curtain panel, folding the curtain fabric and the lining as one. Unfold fabric; tack drapery weight to hem allowance, just above the ruffle. Refold; stitch to make double-fold hem.

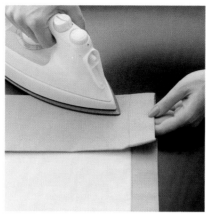

11 Refold top of the panel, folding the curtain fabric and lining as one; press. If curtains will be mounted on pole with elbows, follow step 7 on page 83. If curtain will be mounted on pole with finials, follow steps 4 to 7 on pages 82 and 83. Install curtains as on page 83.

HOW TO MAKE ROD-POCKET CURTAINS WITH A DOUBLE RUFFLE

CUTTING DIRECTIONS

Cut the fabric and lining for curtains as on page 90. Determine the desired finished widths of the upper and lower ruffles, with the lower ruffle 1" (2.5 cm) wider than the upper ruffle. Cut fabric strips for each ruffle on the crosswise grain, with the width of the strips equal to twice the desired finished width plus ½" (1.3 cm). Cut as many strips for each ruffle as necessary for a combined length of two to two-and-one-half times the length to be ruffled; seamed fabric strip for upper ruffle must be exactly the same length as seamed strip for the lower ruffle.

1 Stitch the fabric strips for lower ruffle together in ¼" (6 mm) seams, right sides together; press seams open. Repeat for upper ruffle. Press strip for upper ruffle **(a),** wrong sides together, with raw edge on back side of ruffle strip ½" (1.3 cm) below raw edge on front. Press strip for lower ruffle **(b),** wrong sides together, with raw edge on front side of ruffle strip ½" (1.3 cm) below raw edge on back.

2 Place upper strip on lower strip, right sides up, matching raw edges of outer layers and inner layers; also match raw edges at short end. Pin the top three layers of fabric together at short end.

3 Fold the unpinned layer of lower ruffle strip around upper ruffle strip; pin in place, with raw edges of top two layers matching. Stitch ¼" (6 mm) seam across short end.

4 Repeat steps 2 and 3 for opposite short end. Turn right side out. Fold back front layer of upper ruffle; pin remaining three layers together, with raw edge of lower layer ½" (1.3 cm) above raw edges of middle layers. Baste ¼" (6 mm) from raw edges of middle layers. Attach ruffle and sew curtains as on pages 90 to 92, steps 2 to 11.

HOURGLASS CURTAINS

The name for these curtains is derived from their shape. Hourglass curtains are held taut between rods at the top and bottom and drawn in at the center with a tieback, exposing some of the window glass. Often used on French doors, hourglass curtains rest close to the glass, allowing free movement of the door. Hourglass curtains are usually mounted on narrow sash rods, although wide curtain rods can be used for a different look. Spring-tension rods can also be used when the hourglass curtain is mounted inside the window frame. Decorator sheer fabrics are the best choice for this treatment, especially for doors or windows that are viewed from both sides.

Accurate planning and measuring ensure successful results when making hourglass curtains. To visualize the finished curtain, it is helpful to mark the shape of the hourglass on the window or door, using ribbon or twill tape (page 96). The width of the curtain at the tieback should be between one-third and one-half the width of the window treatment at the top and bottom. Whenever possible, the lower edge of the upper rod and the upper edge of the lower rod should clear the glass by at least ½" (1.3 cm). Be sure to allow room for the rod and the desired heading depth at the top and bottom of the curtain.

French doors (*opposite*) *feature hour-glass curtains for an elegant look.*

Small window *has an hourglass curtain from lightweight cotton fabric for a cozy country look.*

95

HOW TO MEASURE FOR AN HOURGLASS CURTAIN

1 Install rods. Tape a strip of ribbon or twill tape to door or window, outlining desired shape of curtain. Begin at lower outside corner of top rod, angling in desired distance to center, and then out to upper outside corner of bottom rod. Repeat for opposite side.

2 Measure width of curtain across top or bottom; this is referred to as Measurement A. Measure width of curtain across center; this is referred to as Measurement B. Subtract Measurement B from Measurement A; record the difference.

MATERIALS

- Ribbon or twill tape.
- Sheer to lightweight decorator fabric.
- Two sash rods, curtain rods with up to 1¼" (3.2 cm) projection, or spring-tension rods.
- White heavyweight sew-in interfacing; ivory lightweight fusible interfacing, to prevent show-through, optional.

CUTTING DIRECTIONS

Cut the fabric with the length equal to Measurement C plus four times the rod-pocket depth and four times the desired heading depth (page 81) plus 1" (2.5 cm) for turn-under. The cut width of the fabric is equal to two-and-one-half to three times Measurement A, depending on the desired fullness, plus 4" (10 cm) for 1" (2.5 cm) double-fold side hems. Seam fabric widths together, if necessary, using French seams (page 20).

Cut a strip of fabric for the tieback, with the length equal to two times Measurement B plus 1½" (3.8 cm). The cut width of the fabric strip is equal to twice the desired finished width of the tieback plus 1" (2.5 cm).

Cut one strip each of heavyweight sew-in interfacing and optional ivory lightweight fusible interfacing, with the length 1" (2.5 cm) shorter than the cut length of the tieback strip; the cut width is ⅛" (3 mm) narrower than the finished width of the tieback. Fuse the strips together.

3 Measure the length of the ribbon down one angled side; this is referred to as Measurement C. Measure the length of the curtain down the center, measuring from the lower edge of the top rod to the upper edge of the bottom rod; this is referred to as Measurement D. Subtract Measurement D from Measurement C; record the difference.

HOW TO MAKE AN HOURGLASS CURTAIN

1 Seam fabric widths together, if necessary, using French seams (page 20). Press under 1" (2.5 cm) twice on sides of curtain panel; stitch to make double-fold hems, using straight stitch or blindstitch.

2 Press under ½" (1.3 cm) on upper edge. Then press under an amount equal to the rod-pocket depth plus the heading depth; pin.

3 Stitch close to the first fold. Stitch again at the depth of the heading.

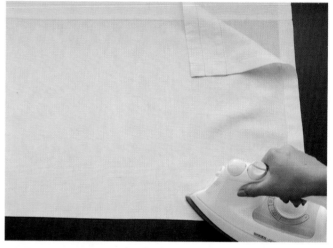

4 Repeat steps 2 and 3 for lower edge of curtain panel. Fold curtain in half crosswise, right sides together, matching top and bottom rod pockets and headings. Press foldline across center of curtain.

5 Divide the difference between Measurement A and Measurement B in half. Then multiply this number by the amount of fullness allowed for the curtain. Measure this distance along pressed fold from one side toward center; pin-mark. Repeat for opposite side. (See inset.)

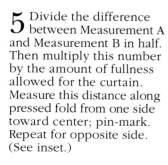

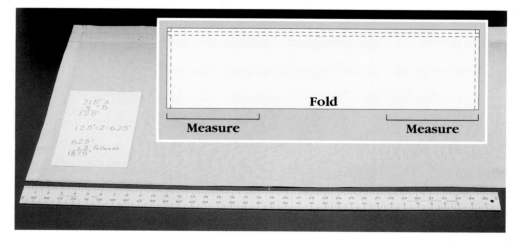

Fold

Measure   **Measure**

(Continued)

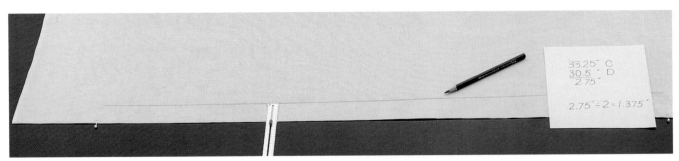

6 Divide the difference between Measurement C and Measurement D in half. Measure in from the fold at pin marks a distance equal to this measurement; mark. Draw a line between pin marks, parallel to the foldline.

7 Extend line to pressed fold at inner edges of side hems, using straightedge, if sash rods or spring-tension rods are used. If rods have up to a 1¼" (3.2 cm) projection, taper line to 4" (10 cm) from side hems. Stitch on marked line, making a long dart.

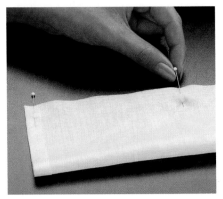

8 Press under ½" (1.3 cm) on one short end of the tieback. Fold the tieback in half lengthwise, right sides together; pin.

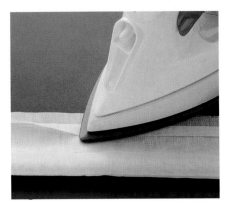

9 Sew a ½" (1.3 cm) seam along the length of tieback; press seam open.

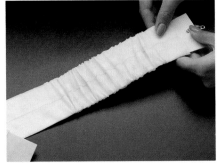

10 Turn tieback right side out, using safety pin or bodkin. Center the seam on back of tieback; press. Insert interfacing strip into tieback (optional ivory interfacing faces front).

11 Insert unfinished end of tieback into pressed end, overlapping ½" (1.3 cm). Slipstitch ends together, making a circular tieback.

12 Install curtain (opposite); check fit. Adjust stitching of dart, if necessary. Trim fabric ½" (1.3 cm) from stitched dart; finish seam, and press. Reinstall curtain.

HOW TO INSTALL AN HOURGLASS CURTAIN
USING RODS WITH BRACKETS

1 Remove rods from brackets; insert top rod into top rod pocket of curtain. Mount top rod in brackets.

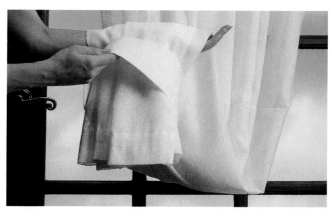

2 Place curtain through tieback. Insert bottom rod into bottom rod pocket.

3 Distribute gathers evenly on rods. Position tieback at center of curtain. Mount bottom rod in brackets, pulling curtain taut.

4 Secure tieback to center of curtain, using concealed safety pin.

HOW TO INSTALL AN HOURGLASS CURTAIN
USING SPRING-TENSION RODS

1 Place curtain through tieback. Remove rubber tips from ends of spring-tension rods. Insert the spring-tension rods in top and bottom rod pockets. Replace rubber tips.

2 Mount rods inside window frame, pulling curtain taut between them; distribute gathers evenly, covering the rubber tips of rods. Center tieback over seam. Secure the tieback to center of curtain, using concealed safety pin.

SPLIT HOURGLASS CURTAINS

Split hourglass curtains form a diamond of open glass at the center of the door or window. Like other hourglass curtains, the shaping is achieved by a dart sewn at the center, hidden under the tieback. The split hourglass is made in two panels, shaped in opposite directions and installed on the same rods at the top and bottom.

MATERIALS

- Sheer to lightweight decorator fabric.
- Two sash rods, rods with up to 1¼" (3.2 cm) projection, or spring-tension rods.
- White heavyweight sew-in interfacing.
- Ivory lightweight fusible interfacing, to prevent show-through of white heavyweight interfacing, optional.
- Thumbtacks or self-adhesive hook and loop tape, for securing tiebacks.

CUTTING DIRECTIONS

Cut the fabric for each curtain panel, with the length equal to the angled side measurement as determined in step 2, opposite, plus four times the depth of the rod pocket plus four times the desired heading depth plus 1" (2.5 cm) for turn-under. The cut width of the fabric for each panel is equal to two-and-one-half to three times the finished width of the panel plus 4" (10 cm) to allow for 1" (2.5 cm) double-fold side hems.

Cut a strip of fabric for each tieback, with the length of the strip equal to two times the center width of one panel plus 1½" (3.8 cm). The cut width of the strip is equal to three times the desired finished width of the tieback. Cut the sew-in and optional fusible interfacing as on page 96.

HOW TO MEASURE FOR A SPLIT HOURGLASS CURTAIN

 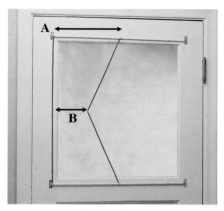 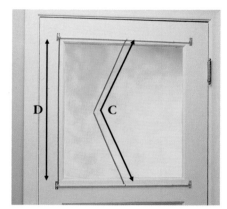

1 Install the rods. Tape a strip of twill tape or ribbon to the window, outlining the desired shape of curtain panels. Begin at lower center of the upper rod, angling out to the desired inner point for tieback, and then in to upper center of the lower rod.

2 Measure the width across top or bottom of one panel; this is referred to as Measurement A. Measure the width of panel across center; this is referred to as Measurement B. Subtract Measurement B from Measurement A; record the difference.

3 Measure length of twill tape or ribbon down angled side; this is referred to as Measurement C. Measure length of curtain down straight side, measuring from lower edge of upper rod to upper edge of lower rod; this is referred to as Measurement D. Subtract Measurement D from Measurement C; record the difference.

HOW TO MAKE A SPLIT HOURGLASS CURTAIN

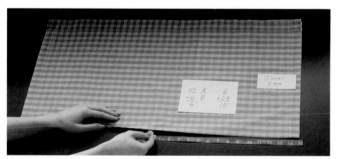 

1 Follow steps 1 to 4 on page 97, for each curtain panel. Multiply the difference between Measurement A and Measurement B, as determined in step 2, above, by the amount of fullness allowed for the curtain. Measure this distance along pressed fold from inner side of the panel toward outer side; pin-mark. Repeat for the second panel.

2 Divide the difference between Measurement C and Measurement D, as determined in step 3, above, in half. Measure from the pressed fold a distance equal to this measurement; draw a line through hemmed edge on outer side to the pin mark, parallel to the foldline.

3 Extend the line from pin mark to pressed fold at hem on inner side of panel; line does not extend into hem allowance. Stitch on marked line, creating a dart through center of each curtain panel. Complete curtain and tiebacks as on page 98, steps 8 to 11.

4 Install curtain as on page 99, steps 1 to 4 for rods with brackets, or steps 1 and 2 for spring-tension rods. Secure tiebacks to outer edges of window frame, using thumbtacks or self-adhesive hook and loop tape. Check fit and finish curtain as on page 98, step 12.

MORE IDEAS FOR HOURGLASS CURTAINS

Angled panels *expose only a small area of glass. The curtains, sewn like single panels of the split hourglass curtain on page 100, are mounted on 1" (2.5 cm) sash rods.*

Hourglass curtain *(below) is stretched horizontally between spring-tension rods in this small window.*

Long tails of ribbon emphasize the high placement of the tieback on this hourglass curtain. This curtain is sewn as on pages 96 to 98, stitching the dart one-third of the way down from the top of the curtain, rather than across the middle.

Triple diamond effect (below) is created by mounting two hourglass curtains (page 95) between two split hourglass panels (page 100). All the panels are mounted on the same tension rods.

DECORATIVE HEADINGS

Flounce heading drapes down over the front of the rod pocket, creating a mock valance. Allow a heading depth of 12" to 16" (30.5 to 40.5 cm). This treatment is suitable only for rods or poles with elbow returns. Sheer fabric may be used for this style in unlined curtains.

Popped heading is created by pulling the layers of the heading apart after inserting the rod into the pocket. Allow a heading depth of 6" to 8" (15 to 20.5 cm); do not press the upper edge of the curtain when turning under the heading and rod-pocket depth. This style may be used for sheer to mediumweight fabrics and may be lined or unlined.

Some simple variations in the headings of rod-pocket curtains can dramatically change their look. For some styles, such as the flounce heading or the popped heading, the variation is achieved by simply increasing the depth of the heading and arranging it after it has been installed. For styles such as the contrasting flounce and the welted heading, a separate facing is seamed to the curtain at the top of the heading. Although the instructions that follow are for lined curtains, the lining may be omitted, if desired, depending on the style of the curtain and the fabric selected.

Contrasting flounce can repeat a fabric that is used in the tieback for a coordinated look. A separate facing of contrasting fabric is sewn to the curtain at the top of the heading. Lining adds body to the heading and prevents show-through when a light-colored fabric is used for the flounce.

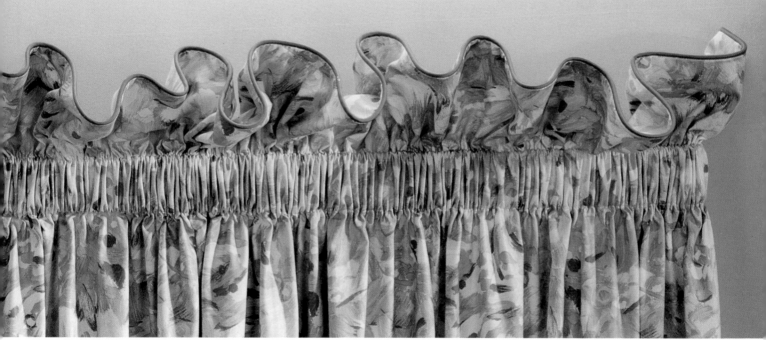

Welted heading, measuring 4" to 6" (10 to 15 cm) deep, droops into dramatic curves above the rod pocket. Contrasting welting is sewn into the seam at the top of the heading between the curtain and the facing. This style is appropriate for mediumweight fabrics and should always be lined.

HOW TO MAKE ROD-POCKET CURTAINS WITH A FLOUNCE OR POPPED HEADING

MATERIALS

- Decorator fabric; lining.
- Drapery weights.
- Curtain rod or pole with elbow returns.

CUTTING DIRECTIONS

Cut the decorator fabric and lining as on page 82; allow for a 12" to 16" (30.5 to 40.5 cm) flounce heading, or a 6" to 8" (15 to 20.5 cm) popped heading.

Flounce heading. Sew curtains as on pages 82 and 83. When installing the curtains, drape the heading toward the front, over the rod pocket, and arrange the gathers.

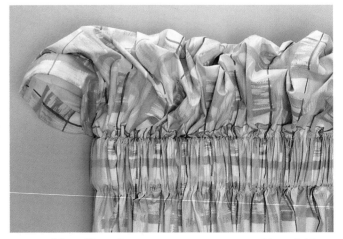

Popped heading. Sew curtains as on pages 82 and 83. Pull layers of heading apart, for a soft, rounded look.

HOW TO MAKE ROD-POCKET CURTAINS WITH A CONTRASTING FLOUNCE

MATERIALS

- Decorator fabric.
- Contrasting decorator fabric, for facing.
- Lining.
- Drapery weights.
- Curtain rod or pole with elbow returns.

CUTTING DIRECTIONS

Cut the decorator fabric for the curtains with the length equal to the desired finished length of the curtains from the top of the curtain rod to the lower edge of the finished curtain plus twice the depth of the hem plus ½" (1.3 cm) for the seam allowance at the top plus the depth of the flounce heading; allow for a 12" to 16" (30.5 to 40.5 cm) flounce heading. Determine the cut width as on page 82.

Cut the fabric for the facing with the length equal to the depth of the heading plus the depth of the rod pocket plus 1" (2.5 cm) for turn-under and seam allowance. The cut width of the facing is the same as the cut width of the decorator fabric.

Cut the lining fabric 5" (12.5 cm) shorter than the decorator fabric. The cut width of the lining is the same as the cut width of the decorator fabric.

1 Seam decorator fabric widths, if necessary, for each curtain panel; repeat for facing and lining panels. At lower edge of curtain panel, press under 4" (10 cm) twice to wrong side; stitch to make double-fold hem. Repeat for hem on lining panel, pressing under 2" (5 cm) twice.

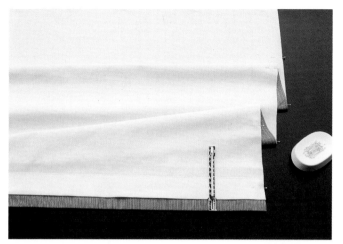

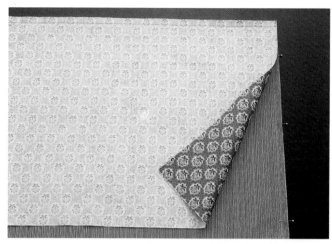

2 Place the curtain panel and the lining panel wrong sides together, matching the raw edges at sides and upper edge; pin. At the bottom, lining panel will be 1" (2.5 cm) shorter than the curtain panel.

3 Pin facing to top of curtain panel, right sides together; if the facing fabric has one-way design, pin the flounce so design is upside down at the upper edge of the curtain panel. Stitch ½" (1.3 cm) seam; press the seam open.

4 Press under 1½" (3.8 cm) twice on sides, folding lining and curtain fabric as one. Open out hem, and trim seam allowance in hem area. Tack drapery weights inside the side hems, about 3" (7.5 cm) from the lower edge. Stitch to make double-fold hems.

5 Press under ½" (1.3 cm) on lower edge of flounce. Turn under facing along seamline; press. Pin flounce to the curtain panel along the lower pressed edge. Mark upper stitching line for rod pocket on facing. Pin along line to keep all layers together.

6 Stitch close to lower pressed edge; stitch again along the marked line, creating rod pocket.

7 Insert the rod or pole through rod pocket, gathering fabric evenly. Mount the rod or pole on brackets, draping heading toward the front, over the rod pocket, and arrange the gathers.

HOW TO MAKE ROD-POCKET CURTAINS
WITH A WELTED HEADING

MATERIALS

- Decorator fabric for curtain and facing.
- Contrasting fabric and ¼" (6 mm) cording, for covered welting.
- Lining fabric.
- Drapery weights.
- Curtain rod or pole set.

CUTTING DIRECTIONS

Cut the decorator fabric, facing, and lining as for rod-pocket curtains with a contrasting flounce (page 106); allow for a 4" to 6" (10 to 15 cm) heading. From contrasting fabric, cut bias fabric strips, 2" (5 cm) wide, to cover the cording for the welting.

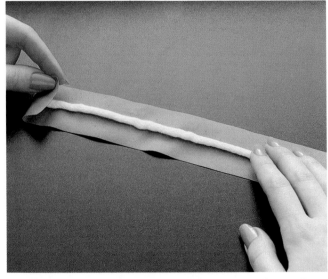

1 Seam the bias fabric strips together. Center the cording on the wrong side of the fabric strip, with the end of cording 1" (2.5 cm) from the end of strip; fold end of the strip back over the cording.

2 Fold the fabric strip around the cording, wrong sides together, matching the raw edges and encasing the end of the cording.

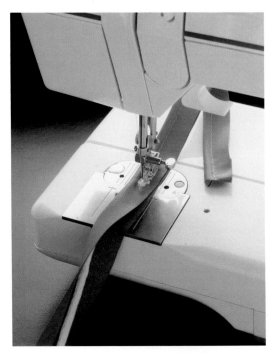

3 Machine-baste close to the cording, using a zipper foot, to create welting.

4 Follow steps 1 and 2 on pages 106 and 107 for contrasting flounce. Stitch the welting to the right side of curtain panel at the upper edge, matching raw edges and stitching over the previous stitches; place the encased end of the welting 3" (7.5 cm) from side of panel. Stop stitching 5" (12.5 cm) from the opposite side of the panel.

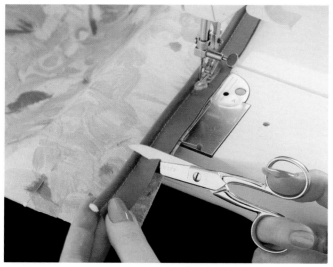

5 Mark the upper edge of the curtain 3" (7.5 cm) from the side; cut the welting 1" (2.5 cm) beyond the mark.

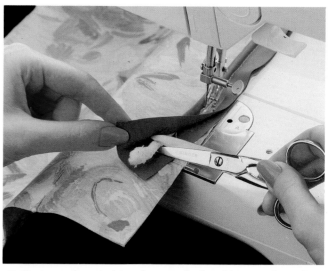

6 Remove the stitching from end of welting, and cut the cording even with the mark on curtain panel.

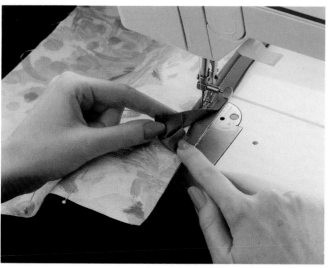

7 Fold the end of fabric strip over the cording, encasing the end of the cording. Finish stitching welting to the curtain panel, ending 3" (7.5 cm) from the side.

8 Follow steps 3 and 4 on page 107 for the contrasting flounce. When stitching side hems, stitch up to welting and secure threads; start stitching again on other side of the welting.

9 Complete the curtains as on page 107, steps 5 and 6. Insert the rod or pole through the rod pocket, gathering the fabric evenly. Mount the rod or pole on brackets; arrange the heading in deep curves as desired.

Valance and cafe curtains, with their casual style, are appropriate for a country bathroom. On a double-hung window, mount the curtain rod for the cafe curtain above the center of the window.

HOW TO SEW A ROD-POCKET CURTAIN
WITH AN ATTACHED VALANCE

MATERIALS

• Fabric.   • Curtain rod.

CUTTING DIRECTIONS

Determine the desired finished length of the curtain from the top of the heading to the hemmed lower edge. Also decide the depths of the rod pocket and the heading (page 81) as well as the hems; a 4" (10 cm) double-fold hem is often used for the curtain panels, and a 2" (5 cm) double-fold hem is used for the valance.

The cut length of the fabric for the curtain panels is equal to the desired finished length of the curtain plus twice the hem depth. Determine the cut width of the fabric for the curtain panels by multiplying the length of the rod by two and one-half; if you are sewing two curtain panels,

divide this measurement by two to determine the cut width of each panel. For each panel, add 6" (15 cm) to allow for two 1½" (3.8 cm) double-fold side hems; if it is necessary to piece fabric widths together, also add 1" (2.5 cm) for each seam.

Determine the desired finished length of the valance from the top of the heading to the hemmed lower edge. The cut length of the fabric for the valance is equal to the desired finished length of the valance plus the depth of the heading and rod pocket, ½" (1.3 cm) for turn-under at the upper edge, and twice the hem depth.

The cut width of the valance is equal to the finished width of the curtain plus 4" (10 cm) for the side hems; also add 1" (2.5 cm) for each seam. If two curtain panels are to be attached to the same valance, base the cut width of the valance on the combined finished width of the curtain panels.

1 Seam the fabric widths and stitch the lower and side hems of the curtain panels and valance as on page 82, steps 1 and 2.

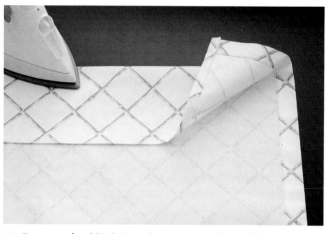

2 Press under ½" (1.3 cm) on upper edge of the valance. Then press under an amount equal to the rod-pocket depth plus heading depth.

3 Place the valance right side down on a flat surface; open out upper fold. Place the curtain panels over valance, right side down, aligning upper edge of curtain with foldline on valance. Refold the upper edge of the valance, encasing upper edge of curtain; pin in place.

4 Stitch rod pocket as on page 83, step 7. Insert rod through rod pocket, gathering fabric evenly; hang curtain.

TIEBACKS

Braided tiebacks *(above) can repeat the design and colors of a braided rug.*

Shirred tiebacks *(left) mimic the effect created at the heading of rod-pocket curtains.*

Many rod-pocket curtains are used with tiebacks that hold the panels in place. Tiebacks offer a decorative opportunity to repeat a design or embellishment used elsewhere in the room. For example, the design of a braided rug can be repeated in a braided tieback, or the shirred effect created by the rod pocket can be repeated in a shirred tieback. You may want to sew fabric bands or galloon lace onto tiebacks with tucked ends, to coordinate with decorative towels, pillows, or curtain details.

Braided or shirred tiebacks can be made from covered cording. Consider the size of the window when choosing the size of the cording. Because these tiebacks are circular, they

Tiebacks with tucked ends *have clean, simple design lines. Above, coordinating fabrics are used for the curtain and tieback. At right, the tieback is trimmed with folded, pressed, and edgestitched bias fabric bands.*

can simply be slipped onto the curtain from the bottom and secured with one hook. For tiebacks with tucked ends, apply mediumweight fusible interfacing to the wrong side of the fabric for added body.

The position of the tiebacks on the window curtain affects the amount of exposed glass as well as the overall look of the curtains. Position tiebacks low to cover more of the window and to visually widen the window. If tiebacks are positioned high, more of the glass is exposed and visual height is added to the window. Also follow these guidelines for positioning the tiebacks on a shower curtain, allowing enough room for easy access to the tub.

TIEBACKS

Tiebacks are not only functional, they are often the focal point of a window treatment. For a stylish touch, they can be shaped in a gentle curve. Welting can be added to accent the edges of shaped tiebacks, perhaps repeating the detailing of a welted heading (page 105). Ruffled tiebacks are the natural choice for ruffled curtains (page 90), but also work well on curtains with flounce headings (page 104).

Tiebacks are often positioned so they divide the curtain panel vertically into thirds. If the tiebacks are positioned one-third of the way from the bottom of the curtains, more window glass remains covered and the window appears wider. If they are positioned one-third of the way from the top, more window glass

Shaped tiebacks (left and below) have a clean, tailored look. They may be sewn with or without welting.

is revealed and the window appears longer. Also consider where to position the tieback in relation to any window details, such as sills or mullions.

Measure for the finished length of the tiebacks after the curtains are made and installed. Generally, the length of each tieback is one-half the total length of the curtain rod plus the projection of the rod. This allows each curtain panel to be pulled back to one-half its width. To visualize how the curtain will look tied back, wrap a cloth tape measure around the curtain panel at the desired tieback height and pull the panel back the desired distance. Angle the tape measure upward toward the outer edge of the curtain where the tieback holder will be placed.

Ruffled tiebacks *(right and below) add a romantic touch. They may have a single or double ruffle.*

HOW TO MAKE BRAIDED TIEBACKS

MATERIALS

- Fabrics in one, two, or three solid colors or prints.
- Cording in desired diameter.
- Sew-on or pin-on tieback rings.

CUTTING DIRECTIONS

Determine the finished circumference of the tieback (page 115). For one braided tieback, cut three lengths of cording, each three times the finished circumference of the tieback; wrap tape around the ends to prevent fraying. Cut three fabric strips, each one-and-one-half times the finished circumference of the tieback; to determine the width of the fabric strips, measure around the cording and add 1" (2.5 cm).

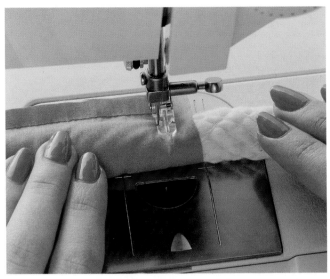

1 Fold one fabric strip around one length of the cording, right sides together, matching the raw edges. Using a zipper foot, stitch loosely along the cording from one end of the fabric strip to the other; do not crowd the cording. Pivot, and stitch across fabric strip, about ½" (1.3 cm) from end of fabric, sewing through middle of cording length.

2 Hold fabric loosely at stitched end; pull the fabric from covered to uncovered end of cording, turning the tube right side out to encase the cording. Cut off the cording just beyond stitched end; discard excess cording. Repeat to cover the remaining cords; three cords are needed for each braided tieback.

3 Pin the three covered cords together, about 1" (2.5 cm) from the stitched ends, using large safety pin. Braid loosely to desired length, keeping seams to back of braid. Measure from end of cords to 1" (2.5 cm) less than desired finished circumference, and pin cords together at that point with another safety pin.

4 Shape the braid into a circle; cut cords at end of braid so they overlap cords at beginning of braid by 1" (2.5 cm). Pull out and cut off 1" (2.5 cm) of cording from each cut end; slide end of fabric tube back over end of the cording.

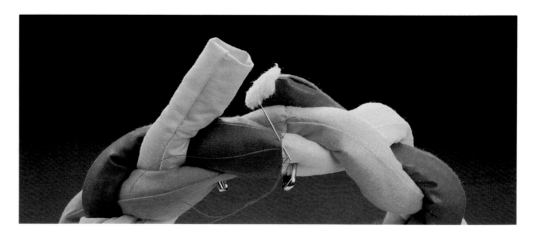

5 Turn under ½" (1.3 cm) of fabric at ends of tubes. Insert stitched ends of the covered cords into open ends of the fabric tubes, overlapping ½" (1.3 cm) and joining ends so braid is continuous; slipstitch. Remove safety pins. Attach a tieback ring.

HOW TO MAKE SHIRRED TIEBACKS

MATERIALS

- Fabric that matches or contrasts with curtain fabric.
- Cording in desired diameter.
- Sew-on or pin-on tieback rings.

CUTTING DIRECTIONS

For each tieback, cut a length of cording equal to three times the finished circumference of the tieback; wrap tape around the ends to prevent fraying. Cut a fabric strip equal to twice the finished circumference of the tieback; to determine the width of the fabric strip, measure around the cording and add 2" (5 cm).

1 Fold the fabric strip in half lengthwise, right sides together, encasing the cording; stitch a ½" (1.3 cm) seam. Stitch across the end of the fabric strip through cording.

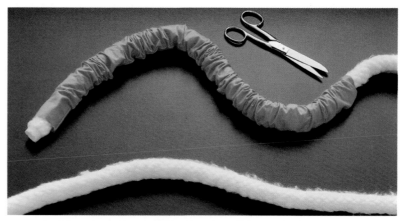

2 Hold fabric loosely at stitched end; pull fabric from the covered to the uncovered end of cording, turning tube right side out to encase the cording and gathering fabric as tube is turned. Cut off and discard excess cording.

3 Sew the ends of the cording together securely.

4 Turn under ½" (1.3 cm) at the end of the fabric tube. Overlap the stitched end of the covered cord; slipstitch in place. Distribute fabric evenly along the cording. Attach a tieback ring.

HOW TO SEW TIEBACKS WITH TUCKED ENDS

MATERIALS

- Fabric that matches or contrasts with the curtain fabric.
- Fusible interfacing.
- Sew-on or pin-on tieback rings.
- Optional embellishments, such as fabric bands (page 113) or galloon lace.

CUTTING DIRECTIONS

For each tieback, cut a fabric strip 1" (2.5 cm) longer than the desired finished length, with the width of the fabric strip equal to twice the desired finished width plus 1" (2.5 cm). Cut a strip of fusible interfacing to the desired finished length and width of the tieback.

1 Center strip of fusible interfacing on the wrong side of fabric strip, and fuse in place, following the manufacturer's directions. The right side of the interfaced area will be the front of the tieback.

2 Apply any desired embellishments to right side of the tieback in the interfaced area, such as the fabric bands (page 113) shown.

3 Fold the tieback in half, right sides together. Stitch ½" (1.3 cm) lengthwise seam, leaving opening for turning. Press seam open.

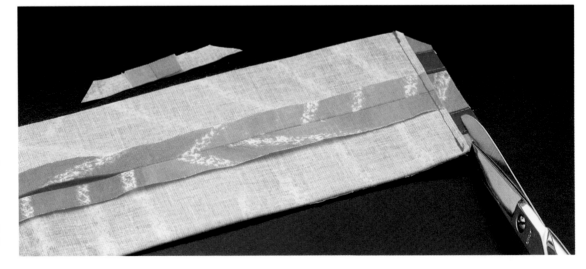

4 Center seam on back of tieback. Stitch ½" (1.3 cm) seams at the ends; trim seam allowances, and clip corners.

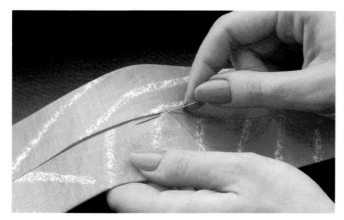

5 Turn the tieback right side out, and press. Slipstitch the opening closed.

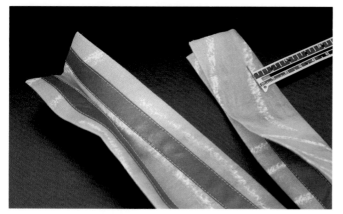

6 Fold one end of the tieback in half, right sides together. Stitch a tuck, 1" (2.5 cm) long and ⅜" (1 cm) from the fold, starting 1" (2.5 cm) from end of tieback. Repeat for opposite end.

7 Flatten the tuck, centering it over the stitches.

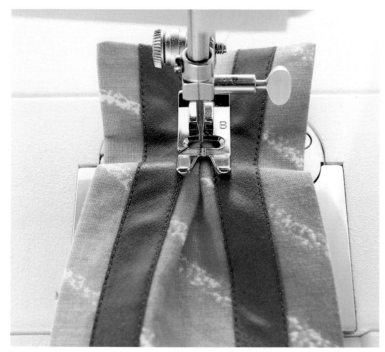

8 Stitch in the ditch of the tuck from the right side, to hold it in place. Repeat for opposite end.

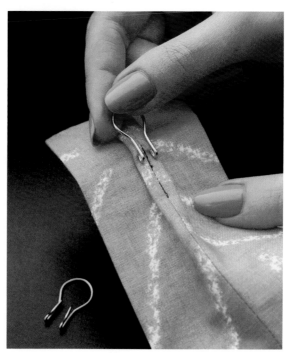

9 Attach pin-on tieback rings as shown. Or stitch sew-on tieback rings in place.

HOW TO MAKE SHAPED TIEBACKS

MATERIALS

- Decorator fabric.
- Fusible polyester fleece or interfacing.
- Cording, for tiebacks with welting.
- Tieback rings, two for each tieback.
- Tieback holders, one for each tieback.
- Flexible curve or curved ruler.

CUTTING DIRECTIONS

Determine the desired finished length of the tiebacks (page 115). Make the pattern for the tiebacks as in steps 1 to 3, below. For each tieback, cut two pieces of decorator fabric and one piece of fusible fleece or interfacing, using the pattern.

If welting is desired, cut bias fabric strips to cover the welting, with the total length of the seamed strips 2" to 3" (5 to 7.5 cm) longer than the distance around the tieback. To determine the cut width of the strips, wrap a tape measure around the cording; the cut width of the strips is equal to the measurement around the cording plus 1" (2.5 cm).

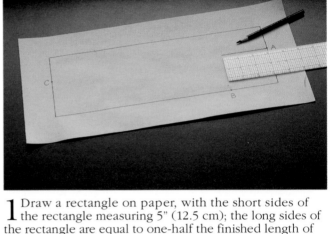

1 Draw a rectangle on paper, with the short sides of the rectangle measuring 5" (12.5 cm); the long sides of the rectangle are equal to one-half the finished length of tieback. Mark Point A on one short side, 3" (7.5 cm) from the lower corner. Mark Point B on the long side 3" (7.5 cm) from the same corner. Mark Point C on the opposite short side, 2" (5 cm) down from upper corner. Draw 3" (7.5 cm) line from Point A parallel to long sides.

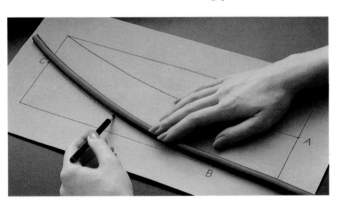

2 Use a flexible curve or a curved ruler to mark a gradual curve for the upper edge of the tieback, connecting the end of the 3" (7.5 cm) line to the upper corner on opposite side of the rectangle. For the lower edge of tieback, draw a curved line from Point C to Point B.

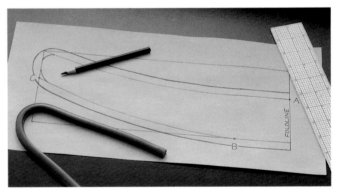

3 Mark center foldline on side with Point A; round corners on the opposite side, for the return. Add ½" (1.3 cm) seam allowances at the upper and lower edges and around the return end.

4 Cut fabric and fusible fleece or interfacing, above. Trim ½" (1.3 cm) from the outer edge of fleece or interfacing; center on wrong side of outer tieback piece, and fuse in place. For tieback without welting, omit steps 5 to 9.

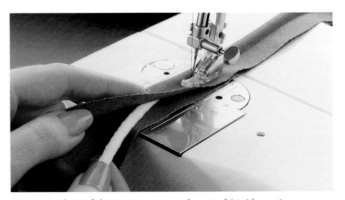

5 Seam bias fabric strips together in ¼" (6 mm) seams. Fold fabric strip over cording, right side out, matching the raw edges. Using zipper foot, machine-baste close to the cording.

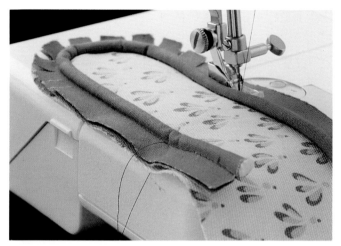

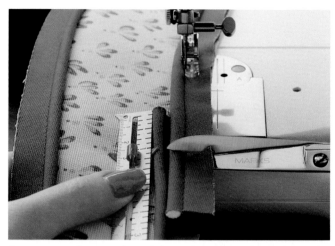

6 Stitch the welting to the right side of tieback, matching raw edges; start 2" (5 cm) from the end of welting in an area of the tieback that will be concealed behind the curtain. To ease welting at the rounded corners, clip seam allowances to basting stitches.

7 Stop stitching 2" (5 cm) from the point where the ends of the welting will meet. Cut off one end of welting so it overlaps the other end by 1" (2.5 cm).

8 Remove the stitching from one end of the welting, and trim the ends of the cording so they just meet.

9 Fold under ½" (1.3 cm) of fabric on overlapping end. Lap it around the other end; finish stitching the welting to the tieback.

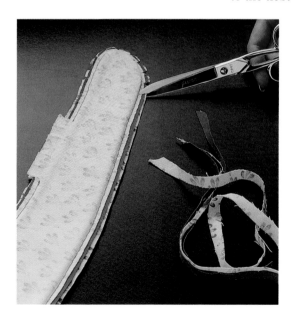

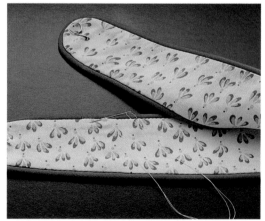

10 Pin the outer tieback and lining pieces right sides together. Stitch ½" (1.3 cm) from raw edges, crowding cording; leave opening for turning. Trim seam allowances. Clip the curved upper and lower edges every ½" (1.3 cm); notch the curves of the return ends.

11 Turn right side out; press. Slipstitch the opening closed. Secure tieback rings to wrong side of tieback, with one ring centered near each end. Attach the tieback to tieback holder (page 10).

HOW TO MAKE RUFFLED TIEBACKS

MATERIALS

- Decorator fabric.
- Fusible interfacing.
- Tieback rings, two for each tieback.
- Tieback holders, one for each tieback.

CUTTING DIRECTIONS

Determine the desired finished length of the tiebacks (page 115). Cut one 3½" (9 cm) fabric strip for each tieback band, with the length of the strip equal to the finished length of the tieback plus 1" (2.5 cm); this gives a finished band width of 1¼" (3.2 cm). Cut a 2½" (6.5 cm) strip of fusible interfacing for each tieback, with the length equal to the finished length of the tieback. Cut the fabric for single or double ruffles as for ruffled curtains on page 91 or 93.

1 Center the interfacing on wrong side of tieback; fuse in place. Press up ⅜" (1 cm) on one long side of tieback.

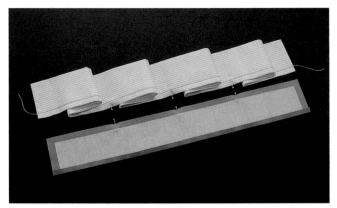

2 Prepare single ruffles as on page 91, steps 1 and 2, or prepare double ruffles as on page 93, steps 1 to 4. Divide ruffle strip and tieback band into fourths; pin-mark.

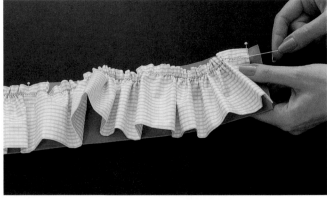

3 Pin the ruffle strip to the unfolded side of the tieback band, right sides together, matching pin marks and raw edges, with ends of ruffle strip ½" (1.3 cm) from ends of the band. Pull up gathering cord on the ruffle to fit band; pin in place. Stitch ½" (1.3 cm) from raw edges.

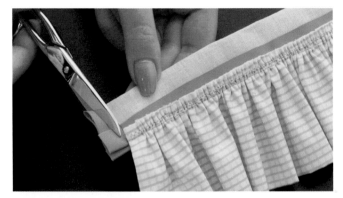

4 Trim seam allowance of the ruffle to ¼" (6 mm). Fold the end of the band in half, wrong sides together, with the folded edge extending ⅛" (3 mm) beyond stitching line. Stitch ½" (1.3 cm) from end, taking care not to catch the ruffle in stitching; trim seam allowances. Repeat for the opposite end.

5 Turn the band right side out, and press; the folded edge extends ⅛" (3 mm) below the stitching line on the back of the band. Pin in place; stitch in the ditch from the right side, catching the folded edge on the back of band. Secure tieback rings as on page 121, step 11; attach the tieback to the tieback holder (page 10).

MORE IDEAS FOR TIEBACKS

Scalloped edge *on a shaped tieback adds a designer touch to a window treatment.*

Knotted men's necktie, *tied in a Windsor knot, holds back a plaid curtain.*

Jute rope *serves as a creative tieback with rustic appeal.*

Scarf *used as a tieback has a soft, carefree look.*

Ribbons with floral nosegay *gather an hourglass curtain.*

Narrow *decorative cord is draped along the upper edge of a scalloped curtain panel, echoing the arc of the scallops. Cord is hand-tacked at the base of each tab or ring.*

Decorative cord gives a window treatment the look of elegance and high style. It can be draped in creative ways to emphasize design lines of the treatment or it can be used for opulent tiebacks. Tassels are the perfect accompaniments for cord embellishments, since they are designed to look like beautifully raveled cord ends. By themselves, tassels can be used for decorative accents in various ways.

Decorative cords and tassels are available in a variety of colors and sizes as well as fiber contents. Some cords are made of decorative threads wrapped around a plain cotton core and then twisted into a rope. Other twisted rope styles are made entirely of decorative threads.

Purchased cord and tassel tiebacks, while impressive, can also be very expensive. Decorative cord can be purchased in precut lengths, called *chair ties,* with attached tassels at the ends; however, the length is not adjustable. As an attractive alternative, cords that are made entirely of decorative threads can be successfully raveled to create self tassels.

To create self tassels, purchase about 12" (30.5 cm) of extra decorative cord for each tassel. Bind the cord with heavy thread 3" to 4" (7.5 to 10 cm) from the end, and ravel the ends. Also ravel a 6" to 8" (15 to 20.5 cm) length of cord, keeping the sets of thread separated. Steam press all raveled cord lengths to straighten the threads. Layer the loose sets of thread, and place the raveled cord end over the layered threads, aligning the ends. Wrap the layered threads evenly around the cord, and bind with heavy thread just above the first binding. Fold all threads down over the cord end, and bind again, 3/4" (2 cm) below the top of the tassel. Wrap gimp or narrow braid over the binding.

Cords that do not ravel attractively can be given fringe end caps. Bind the cord with heavy thread close to the end. Wrap a fringe with a decorative heading twice around the cord, turning the cut end under. Secure with hand stitching.

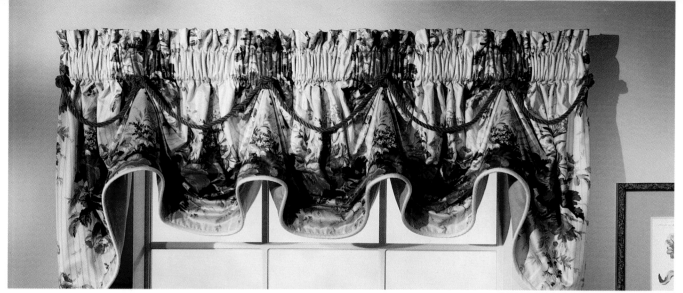

Decorative cord is draped between the bells of a gathered pickup valance to emphasize the curved lines of the swags. Cord can match or coordinate with the welting at the lower edge. A knot tied in the cord at the top of each bell is hand-stitched to the valance, and the ends of the cords are finished with self tassels or end caps.

Decorative cord is glued along the upper edge of a pleated valance, using hot glue. Matching tassels are hung at outer front corners.

Tassels are attached at the bottom of each row of rings on a butterfly Roman shade for a more elegant look. Lower folds are hand-tacked together to support the weight of the tassels.

Tieback curtains are secured with a length of decorative cord. The cord ends are finished with fringe end caps or self tassels.

Top Treatments

BIAS SWAGS

This bias-cut, lined version of the popular swag is easy to make and drapes gracefully. The pattern for the swag is made from one-fourth of a circle. Make a swag with a soft, airy look, using a decorator sheer fabric for the outer fabric and the lining. Or, for a more formal, traditional look, the swag can be made from a mediumweight decorator fabric and trimmed with a bullion fringe along the curved edge.

To hang the swags, attach either clip-on or sew-on rings to the upper edge and slide the rings onto a decorator pole. To keep the rings from shifting, apply a small amount of floral adhesive clay or poster putty to the inside of each ring along the top.

The instructions that follow are based on one-fourth of a circle with a 42" (107 cm) radius. This results in a swag that drapes nicely for a 36" (91.5 cm) width, with a 20" (51 cm) length at the center. Swags sewn this size can be used on poles a few inches (2.5 cm) shorter or longer than 36" (91.5 cm) by varying the spacing between the rings on the pole. When the pole is longer, the draped swag will be shorter at the center; when the pole is shorter, the swag will drape longer. Different sizes may be made by basing the swag pattern on a circle with a larger or smaller radius.

Over large windows, you may want to hang two or more swags, overlapping them, if desired. The swags can be used alone or in combination with another style. Hang swags over an undertreatment with a pole that has a deeper projection, and mount the pole for the swags high enough to hide the undertreatment's upper edge.

Bias swags *may be made from sheer or mediumweight fabric. Opposite, sheer swags are hung side by side. The swags below, trimmed with bullion fringe, are overlapped at the center.*

MATERIALS (for one swag)

- 1¼ yd. (1.15 m) mediumweight decorator fabric and 1¼ yd. (1.15 m) drapery lining; or 2½ yd. (2.3 m) decorator sheer fabric.
- 2 yd. (1.85 m) bullion fringe, optional.
- Decorator pole.
- Clip-on or sew-on drapery rings; 10 rings work well for hanging a single swag on 36" (91.5 cm) pole.

CUTTING DIRECTIONS

Make the pattern for the swag (below). For each swag, cut one piece from decorator fabric and one piece from lining, or cut two pieces from sheer fabric; position the pattern so the straight edges of the pattern are on the straight of grain. When cutting more than one swag, cut a single layer of fabric at a time, for economical use of the fabric.

HOW TO MAKE THE PATTERN FOR A BIAS SWAG

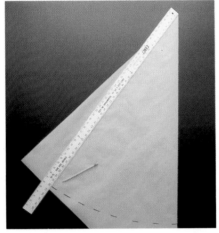

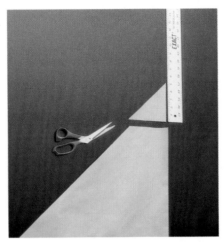

1 Cut 42" (107 cm) square of paper; fold it in half diagonally. Using a straightedge and pencil, draw an arc between square corner and fold, marking the lower edge of swag. Cut on marked line through both layers.

2 Mark the folded edge 5" (25.5 cm) from upper point. Draw a line from mark to opposite edges, perpendicular to fold. Cut on marked line.

3 Fold under 2" (5 cm) on the long straight edges. At lower edge, trim area that is folded under, following the curve. Unfold pattern.

HOW TO SEW A BIAS SWAG

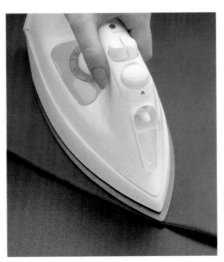

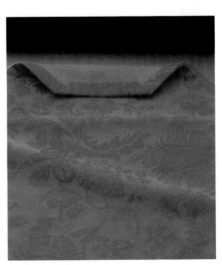

1 Cut fabric (above). Pin decorator fabric and lining, with right sides together, along curved edge. Stitch ½" (1.3 cm) seam; press open.

2 Turn the swag right side out. Press the curved edge.

3 Press under 1" (2.5 cm) twice on the long straight sides, folding the decorator fabric and lining together; stitch hem. Repeat at the upper edge. Apply fringe to curve, if desired.

HOW TO HANG A BIAS SWAG

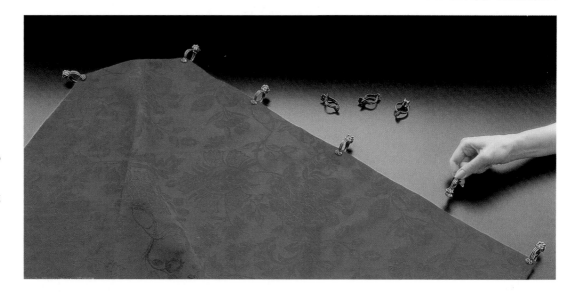

1 Attach 10 rings to the upper straight edges of the swag, positioning one ring at each end, one at each inner corner, and remaining six rings evenly spaced between the ends and corners.

2 Hang rings on mounted decorator pole. Arrange swag to desired width and length; arrange folds of fabric for desired look.

3 Apply floral adhesive clay or poster putty to inside of rings, along the top, if necessary to keep rings from shifting.

Overlapped swags. Attach the rings to upper straight edges of swags as in step 1, above, except overlap swags so two of the rings are attached to both swags; a total of 18 rings is used for mounting two overlapped swags.

ROD-POCKET SWAGS

This softly gathered swag valance is a versatile top treatment that can be styled in a variety of ways. For country charm or soft femininity, sew a ruffle to the lower edge. Elegant fabric and bullion fringe (page 137) create a more formal look. The valance can fall in one deep, graceful swag or two swags with equal depths. For yet another look, the valance can be divided to create a triple swag with two equal swags on either side of a third, deeper swag (page 136).

Regardless of the size of the valance or the number of swags, the valance is constructed from a half circle of fabric. Surprisingly, the straight edge of the half circle actually becomes the lower curved edge of the valance to which the ruffle or fringe is attached. The heading and rod pocket of the valance are sewn along the curve of the half circle. To avoid seams, the length of the straight edge should not exceed twice the width of the decorator fabric.

MATERIALS

- Twill tape or ribbon.
- Decorator fabric for valance; the amount needed is equal to the length of the twill tape or ribbon, as determined at right, plus twice the depth of the heading and rod pocket, plus 1" (2.5 cm). Additional fabric is needed for the optional ruffle.
- Lining; the amount needed is equal to the length of the twill tape or ribbon, as determined at right, plus twice the depth of the heading and rod pocket, plus 1" (2.5 cm).
- Curtain rod or pole set.
- Cord, such as pearl cotton, for gathering.

HOW TO MEASURE FOR A ROD-POCKET SWAG

Install the curtain rod or pole. Drape a length of twill tape or ribbon from the rod, simulating the desired shape at the lower edge of the valance. If more than one swag is desired, tie the tape or ribbon into the desired position for each swag. Do not include the width of the ruffle or trim in the depth of the swags. Measuring from the bottom of the rod, measure the length of the twill tape or ribbon.

Rod-pocket swags may have either a single or double ruffle and may have one or two swags, as shown opposite and at right.

CUTTING DIRECTIONS

Determine the depth of the heading and rod pocket (page 81). Fold the decorator fabric in half crosswise; trim the selvages. Mark an arc, using a straightedge and pencil, measuring from the outer edge at the fold, a distance equal to one-half the measured length of the lower edge of the valance plus the depth of the heading and rod pocket plus ½" (1.3 cm). Cut on the marked line through both layers. Cut the lining to the same size.

For the ruffle, cut fabric strips on the crosswise grain of the fabric, with the width of the fabric strips equal to twice the desire finished width of the ruffle plus 1" (2.5 cm). Cut as many fabric strips as necessary for a combined length of two to two-and-one-half times the measured length of the twill tape or ribbon (page 133).

HOW TO SEW A SINGLE ROD-POCKET SWAG

1 Stitch the fabric strips for ruffle together in ¼" (6 mm) seams, right sides together. Press the seams open. Fold ends of strips in half lengthwise, right sides together; stitch across ends in ¼" (6 mm) seams. Turn right side out; press.

2 Zigzag over a cord within ½" (1.3 cm) seam allowance, stitching through both layers of ruffle strip.

3 Divide ruffle and straight edge of valance into fourths or eighths; pin-mark, placing outer pins of valance ½" (1.3 cm) from raw edges. Pin ruffle along straight edge of the valance, right sides together, matching raw edges and pin marks; pull the cord, gathering fabric to fit between the pins. Stitch ruffle to valance a scant ½" (1.3 cm) from the raw edges.

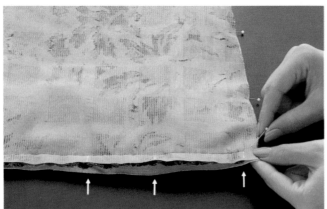

4 Mark ½" (1.3 cm) seam allowance and the depths of heading and rod pocket (page 81) on wrong side of valance fabric (arrows), at each end of straight edge. Pin valance to lining, right sides together, matching raw edges.

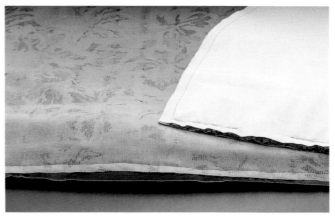

5 Stitch valance to lining in ½" (1.3 cm) seam, stitching with valance faceup. Leave an opening for the rod pocket at each end of the straight edge, and an opening near the center of the straight edge for turning.

6 Press the lining seam allowance toward the lining. Trim the corners diagonally.

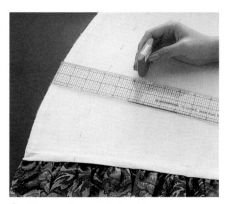

7 Turn valance right side out; press seamed edges. Stitch the center opening closed. Mark chalk lines for depth of heading and depth of rod pocket on curved edge of valance. Pin layers together. Stitch on marked lines.

8 Insert the curtain rod or pole into the rod pocket, gathering fabric evenly. Install rod on brackets. Adjust the folds of valance as desired.

HOW TO SEW A DOUBLE ROD-POCKET SWAG

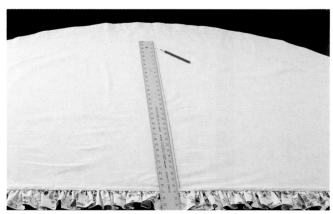

1 Follow steps 1 to 7, opposite. Place valance facedown on flat surface. Divide the lower straight edge, between the rod pockets at ends, into two equal parts; mark ½" (1.3 cm) above seam. Divide upper curved edge into two equal parts. Holding straightedge at marks, draw a line from lower edge, between marks, to a point 2" (5 cm) below the rod pocket.

2 Cut a length of cord, such as pearl cotton, twice the length of the marked line plus 4" (10 cm). Using zigzag stitch of medium length and narrow width, stitch over the cord down left side of line, beginning 2" (5 cm) below the rod pocket, to end of the line; take care not to catch the cord in stitching. Leave needle down in the fabric to right of cord; pivot.

3 Continue stitching over the cord on opposite side of the line toward upper edge, taking care not to catch cord in stitching.

4 Secure stitches at top of line by stitching in place over both cords, using wide zigzag stitch.

5 Follow step 8, above. Draw up gathering cords to desired height; tie cords. Adjust gathers and folds of the valance.

MORE IDEAS FOR ROD-POCKET SWAGS

Single swag (left) without a ruffle is sewn with a popped heading as on page 106. The swag is lined with matching fabric.

Fringe-trimmed swag (opposite) is made from an elegant jacquard fabric for a formal look.

Triple swag (below) is trimmed with tassel fringe instead of a ruffle. The swag has a 2" (5 cm) heading and a 3" (7.5 cm) rod pocket. Follow the steps for a double swag on page 135, except divide the lower straight edge between rod pockets into three parts; also pin-mark upper curved edge about 5" (12.5 cm) from each end, and divide remaining space into three parts. If window sections are unequal, divide spaces for swags in proportion to the window sections.

BUTTONED SWAGS

Top off a simple window treatment with an easy-to-sew buttoned swag valance. The valance is made up of two parts: a shirred fabric sleeve that covers the rod, and a swag that buttons onto the sleeve.

The swagged fabric has one-and-one-half times fullness. Additional fabric is allowed for the draped fabric at the ends. The number of buttons and the distance between them varies with the width of the treatment. On a 36" (91.5 cm) window, use four buttons, creating three swoops; for a wider 60" (152.5 cm) window, it works well to use five buttons, creating four swoops.

Choose a mediumweight decorator fabric that can support the weight of the buttoned treatment, yet will drape nicely between the buttons. Since the swag is lined with self-fabric, avoid patterns that will show through the outer layer, because sunlight can cause patterns to show through more noticeably.

The fabric for both the sleeve and the swag may be cut on the crosswise grain, piecing widths of fabric together to achieve the necessary size. Sometimes, the sleeve and swag may be railroaded (page 21) to eliminate the need for seaming. Railroading can only be used for solid-colored fabrics or patterned fabrics that can be turned sideways, making it inappropriate for fabrics with one-way designs like stemmed flowers or birds.

To prevent an undertreatment from showing in the swooped areas of the swag, the curtain rod for the swag should be mounted so the lower edge of the rod is at least 7" (18 cm) above the under-treatment rod.

HOW TO SEW A BUTTONED SWAG

MATERIALS

- Decorator fabric.
- Curtain rod, 2½" (6.5 cm) wide. If used with an under-treatment, the rod should have a return, or projection, deep enough to clear under-treatment.
- Decorative buttons.
- Small, flat buttons, for reinforcement on the wrong side.

CUTTING DIRECTIONS

For the rod sleeve, cut a fabric strip 7½" (19.3 cm) wide, piecing the strip as necessary to measure two and one-half to three times the length of the curtain rod. If using a wall-mount rod, the 7½" (19.3 cm) fabric strip should be two and one-half to three times the combined length of the rod and the depth of the rod return, or projection.

For the swag, cut a fabric rectangle, 33" (84 cm) wide, piecing it as necessary to measure one and one-half times the rod length plus 45" (115 cm); this allows for the swoops between the buttons and the draped fabric at the sides of the swag.

1 Press under ½" (1.3 cm) twice on the short ends of the fabric strip for the rod sleeve; stitch, to make ½" (1.3 cm) double-fold hems.

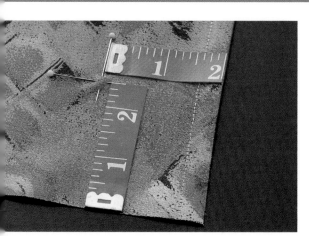

2 **For a spring-tension rod.** Mark a point for the button placement at each end of fabric for the sleeve, measuring 2½" (6.5 cm) from lower edge and 2" (5 cm) from hemmed edge.

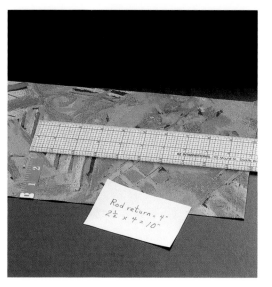

2 **For a wall-mount rod.** Mark a point for button placement at each end of fabric for sleeve, measuring 2½" (6.5 cm) from lower edge and measuring from each hemmed edge a distance equal to two and one-half times the depth of the rod return, or projection.

(Continued)

3 Divide the remaining length between the placement marks equally into desired number of swoops; mark the placement for the buttons, 2½" (6.5 cm) up from the lower edge.

4 Sew a button at each mark, positioning a reinforcement button on wrong side of fabric and a decorative button on right side. Sew through both of the buttons at one time; form a thread shank under the decorative button if it does not have a shank.

5 Fold fabric strip for sleeve in half, right sides together. Stitch ½" (1.3 cm) seam on the long edge; press seam open.

6 Turn the sleeve right side out, centering seam on back of sleeve. Buttons will be at or near lower edge.

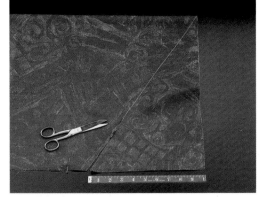

7 Fold fabric for swag in half lengthwise, right sides together, with fold at top; pin long raw edges together at bottom. On the lower edge of swag, measure 10" (25.5 cm) from ends; mark. At each end, draw a line from mark on lower edge to end of fold at top; cut away triangular section.

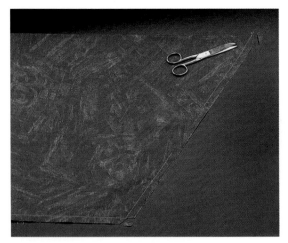

8 Sew ½" (1.3 cm) seam around the ends and lower edge of swag, leaving an opening for turning on one short end; trim corners.

9 Turn swag right side out; press. Stitch opening closed. On fold, measure 22" (56 cm) from each end of swag; mark placement for vertical buttonholes, with upper end of buttonhole ½" (1.3 cm) from the fold.

10 Divide the remaining length between marks equally into desired number of swoops; mark buttonholes. At all placement marks on swag, sew buttonholes large enough to accommodate the decorative buttons.

11 Measure a 2" (5 cm) distance below each buttonhole; fold in half as shown, making 1" (2.5 cm) tuck. Secure tucks by hand-stitching them in place, or use machine bar tacks.

HOW TO HANG A BUTTONED SWAG ON A SPRING-TENSION ROD

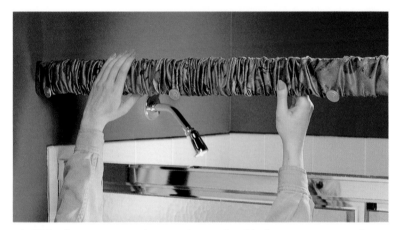

1 Slide sleeve onto spring-tension rod, with the seam centered on back of rod and the buttons at or near lower edge. Mount rod at desired height. Distribute fullness evenly so the spaces between the buttons are equal.

2 Button the swag onto shirred sleeve. Arrange the swoops between the buttons, draping the fabric as desired. Arrange the fabric at each end of the swag.

HOW TO HANG A BUTTONED SWAG ON A WALL-MOUNT ROD

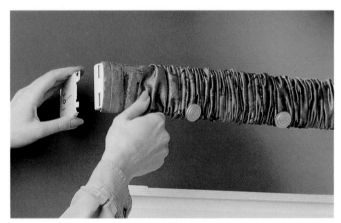

1 Mount brackets on wall at desired location. Slide sleeve onto curtain rod, with seam centered on the back of the rod and buttons about ¼" (6 mm) from the lower edge. Mount the curtain rod.

2 Slide ends of sleeve onto brackets; arrange the shirred sleeve so first and last buttons are located ½" (1.3 cm) from corners on the face of the rod. Hang and arrange the swag as in step 2, above.

The simplicity of scarf swags makes them a favorite informal top treatment. In this method, the shaping of the swag is achieved by cutting out wedges of excess fullness from a length of fabric at each point where the swag crosses a swag holder. The swag is then constructed by sewing the angled pieces together and adding a lining. Simply fanfold the swag along the seams and drape it over the swag holders, to make hanging the swag virtually foolproof. Make swags that drape into a single swoop or into multiple swoops, adding poufs at the top of the side panels, if desired. This scarf swag uses the full width of the fabric and can be either self-lined or lined in a contrasting fabric.

Swag holders are available in several styles, including medallions and scarf rings; decorative tieback holders and holdbacks may also be used (page 10). Mount the holders in the desired locations at the top of the window before beginning the project, and measure for the treatment using twill tape.

Scarf swags *can be sewn in many variations. Above, a swag with a single swoop is held in place with scarf rings. Below, a swag with multiple swoops drapes over swag holders.*

MATERIALS

- Swag holders; one swag holder is needed at each upper corner of the window for a swag with a single swoop, and one holder is needed for each additional swoop.

- Twill tape.

- Decorator fabric for swag, length determined as on page 144, step 1, for swag with single swoop, or as on page 146, step 1, for swag with multiple swoops.

- Matching or contrasting fabric for lining, length equal to decorator fabric.

Scarf swag with poufs
(opposite) is an easy variation of a basic swag. To make the poufs, simply add extra length to the side panels; then fold and tie the poufs in place.

143

HOW TO MEASURE FOR A SCARF SWAG
WITH A SINGLE SWOOP

1 Mount swag holders in desired locations. Drape a length of twill tape over the holders as shown, extending to longest points of tapered sides and stretching straight across top of window. This will be the finished length on the upper edge of the swag.

2 Drape a second length of twill tape over the holders as shown, extending to shortest points of tapered sides and dipping to lowest point desired at center of swoop. This will be the finished length on the lower edge of the swag. Mark both tapes at holders.

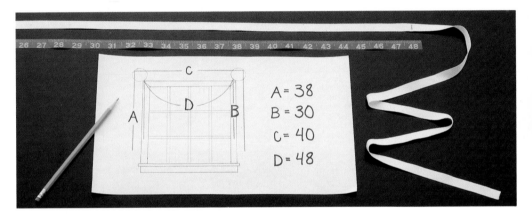

3 Measure and record the lengths of the tape for each section. Measurement A is from the long point to the holder, Measurement B is from the short point to the holder, Measurement C is the distance straight across between the holders, and Measurement D is the length of the swoop between the holders.

A = 38
B = 30
C = 40
D = 48

HOW TO MAKE A SCARF SWAG WITH A SINGLE SWOOP

1 Cut the full width of the fabric, with the length equal to Measurement D plus two times Measurement A plus 3" (7.5 cm) for seam allowances. Measure from each end of the fabric a distance equal to Measurement A plus 1" (2.5 cm). Cut the fabric perpendicular to the selvage at these points.

2 Turn one end piece completely around, if using fabric with an obvious one-way design, so upward direction on both ends points toward the middle; when hung, the design will face in correct direction on end pieces. Label tops of each end piece.

3 Subtract Measurement B from Measurement A. Mark a point on the inside edge of one end piece this distance from the lower cut edge. Draw a line from this point to the lower outside corner; cut away triangular wedge. Repeat for other end piece, cutting angle in opposite direction.

4 Subtract Measurement C from Measurement D; divide this measurement in half. Mark a point on upper edge of the center piece this distance from outer edge. Draw a line from this point to lower corner; cut away triangular wedge. Repeat for opposite side of center piece.

5 Cut lining, using swag pieces as patterns; label tops of lining pieces. Stitch swag pieces together in ½" (1.3 cm) seams, easing to fit; repeat for the lining pieces. Press the seams open.

6 Pin the lining to swag, right sides together. Stitch a ½" (1.3 cm) seam around all sides, leaving an opening along upper edge for turning. Trim corners diagonally. Press lining seam allowance toward the lining.

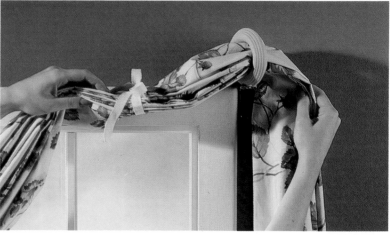

7 Turn the swag right side out; press seamed edges. Slipstitch opening closed.

8 Fanfold swag along seamlines; tie folds with twill tape. Hang swag through scarf ring or over medallion-style scarf holder or tieback holder. Arrange folds in swag and sides as desired. Remove twill tape.

HOW TO MEASURE FOR A SCARF SWAG
WITH MULTIPLE SWOOPS

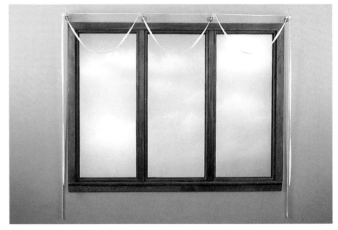

1 Mount swag holders in desired locations. Drape a length of twill tape over the holders as shown, extending to longest points of tapered sides, stretching straight across top of window. This will be the finished length on the top of the swag.

2 Drape a second length of twill tape over the holders, as shown, extending to shortest points of tapered sides, dipping to lowest point desired at center of each swoop. This will be the finished length on the bottom of the swag. Mark both tapes at holders.

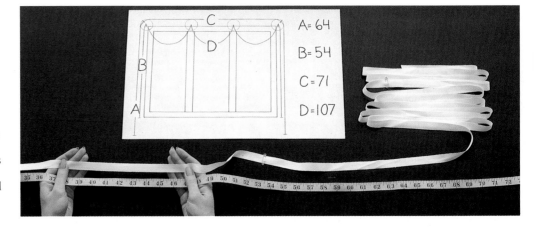

3 Measure and record the lengths of the tape for each section. Measurement A is from the long point to the holder, Measurement B is from the short point to the holder, Measurement C is the distance straight across between the holders, and Measurement D is the total length of all the swoops between end holders.

A = 64

B = 54

C = 71

D = 107

HOW TO MAKE A SCARF SWAG WITH MULTIPLE SWOOPS

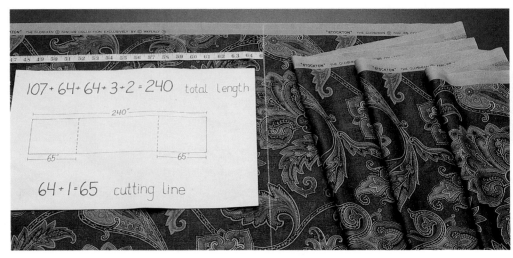

107 + 64 + 64 + 3 + 2 = 240 total length

240"

65"   65"

64 + 1 = 65 cutting line

1 Cut the full width of fabric, with length equal to Measurement D plus two times Measurement A plus 1" (2.5 cm) for each swoop plus an additional 2" (5 cm). Measure from each end of the fabric a distance equal to Measurement A plus 1" (2.5 cm). Cut the fabric perpendicular to the selvage at these points. Follow steps 2 and 3 on pages 144 and 145 for swag with single swoop.

2 Measure the length of the center section; divide this measurement into number of swoops in the swag. Mark the center section into lengths of this size; cut the fabric perpendicular to selvages at these points.

3 Subtract Measurement C from Measurement D. Divide this measurement by the number of swoops in the swag; then divide this number in half. Mark a point on upper edge of one swoop piece this distance from outer edge. Draw a line from this point to lower corner; cut away triangular wedge. Repeat for opposite side of swoop piece. Cut identical wedges from each remaining swoop piece. Complete swag as on page 145, steps 5 to 8.

HOW TO MAKE A SCARF SWAG WITH POUFS

1 Cut the fabric, following step 1 on page 144 for swag with single swoop or step 1, opposite, for swag with multiple swoops, adding 16" to 20" (40.5 to 51 cm) for each pouf. Measure from each end of fabric a distance equal to Measurement A plus length allowed for one pouf plus 1" (2.5 cm). Cut fabric perpendicular to the selvage at these points. Turn one end panel around as on page 144, step 2 (bottom), if using fabric with one-way design.

2 Trim wedges from the end pieces, as on page 145, step 3. Then follow steps 4 to 8 on page 145 for a swag with a single swoop or steps 2 and 3, above, for a swag with multiple swoops; keep folds tied. Tie another piece of twill tape around the fanfolded fabric 16" to 20" (40.5 to 51 cm) below swag holder. Raise tied fabric to the swag holder bracket; knot securely. Fan out fabric to form pouf. Remove upper twill tape.

SHIRRED SWAGS

Less formal than a traditional swag, this lined, pole-mounted swag is easy to make. Shirring tape, stitched to a straight fabric panel, creates the swag with jabots, or side panels. The jabots on this treatment hang in a loose, unstructured style and are stapled in place to conceal the shirring. Welting, inserted at the edges of the swag, adds a finishing touch.

Mount the swag 2" to 3" (5 to 7.5 cm) above the window frame to avoid covering too much of the window. The instructions that follow are for jabots approximately 28" (71 cm) long at the longest point; this length may vary, depending on the amount of shirring.

For best results, select a fabric with a nondirectional print, so that the fabric can be run horizontally across the width of the window, or *railroaded* (page 21). This allows the swag to be constructed without piecing fabric widths together.

MATERIALS

- Decorator fabric.
- Lining.
- 2½ yd. (2.3 m) two-cord shirring tape that gathers to at least four times fullness.
- 5⁄32" (3.8 mm) cording, for welting.
- Wood pole, finials, and keyhole support brackets.

CUTTING DIRECTIONS

Determine the cut length of the fabric panel by measuring the length of the mounting pole and adding 49" (125 cm) to this measurement for the jabots and seam allowances. Cut the fabric and the lining to this length. Trim the outer fabric and the lining to 44" (112 cm) in width. For the welting, cut bias fabric strips 1⅝" (4 cm) wide; piece lengths together as necessary for the measurement determined for the cording in step 1, below.

HOW TO MAKE A SHIRRED SWAG

1 Measure pole length. Center and pin-mark this distance on upper edge of rectangle cut from outer fabric. Measure remaining distance around rectangle, from pin mark to pin mark; cut cording for welting to this measurement plus 1" (2.5 cm). Make welting as on page 108, steps 1 to 3.

2 Pin welting to right side of outer fabric, matching raw edges and extending ends of welting ½" (1.3 cm) beyond pin marks; clip the welting at the corners. Remove the stitching from the welting for ½" (1.3 cm) at the ends; remove cording up to pin mark.

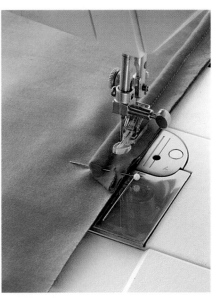

3 Stitch welting to the outer fabric, using zipper foot; fold over ½" (1.3 cm) of welting fabric at ends.

(Continued)

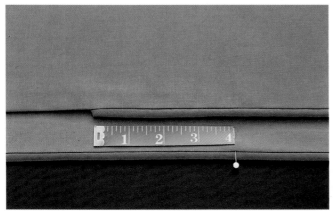

4 Pin lining and outer fabric right sides together; stitch around all four sides close to the previous stitching, leaving a 12" (30.5 cm) opening at center of upper edge. Trim corners diagonally; turn right side out. Press, folding in seam allowances at center opening. Fold panel in half, aligning upper and lower edges; pin-mark lower edge of panel on lining 4" (10 cm) out from end of welting.

5 Position shirring tape diagonally on lining from end of welting to pin mark on lower edge of panel; turn under 1" (2.5 cm) at ends. Use pin to pull out cords. Stitch tape next to cords, through all layers.

6 Knot cords at upper edge of panel; at lower edge, pull evenly on the cords to shirr fabric. Tie off, leaving long tails.

7 Hold pole firmly against the table; using pencil, draw a line on pole where it touches the table.

8 Center the swag on pole, aligning upper edge to marked line on pole; staple in place.

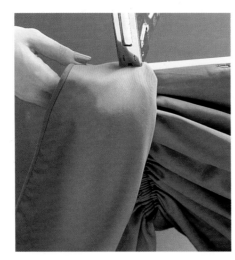

9 Pinch jabot fabric 2" to 4" (5 to 10 cm) from upper edge; pull fabric up to pole and staple in place, concealing shirring tape. Secure the finials to pole.

10 Install pole. Adjust length of shirring, if desired; cut off excess cord length.

MORE IDEAS FOR SHIRRED SWAGS

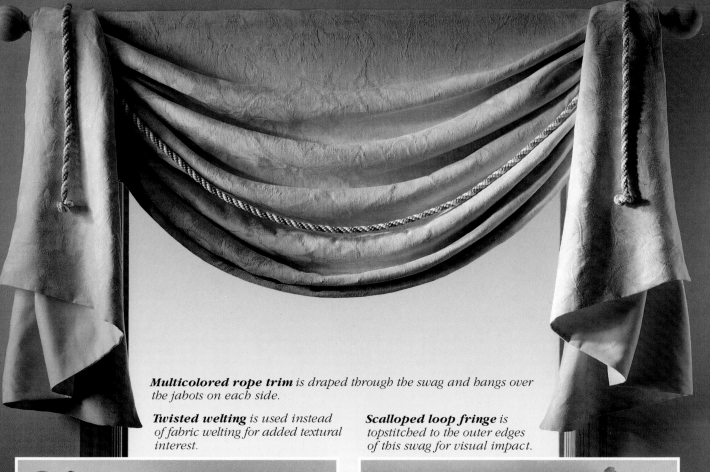

Multicolored rope trim *is draped through the swag and hangs over the jabots on each side.*

Twisted welting *is used instead of fabric welting for added textural interest.*

Scalloped loop fringe *is topstitched to the outer edges of this swag for visual impact.*

TAILORED SWAGS

This simple swag is created by mounting a fabric panel to a board and using fabric tabs on each end to hold the swagged fabric in place. The tailored look is achieved by fan folding the fabric panel before mounting it to the board. The fabric at the ends of the panel drapes to form jabots, or side panels. These jabots can be cut straight or tapered at the lower edge. Use this top treatment alone or with blinds, pleated shades, or sheer curtain panels.

This swag works best as an outside mount, positioned about 2" to 3" (5 to 7.5 cm) above the woodwork. If the board is mounted higher, be sure to make the tabs that support the swags long enough to conceal the woodwork. Mount the swag on a 1 × 3 board if there is no undertreatment. With an undertreatment, use a mounting board that will project out from the window frame far enough for the swag to clear the undertreatment by 1" to 2" (2.5 to 5 cm). The length of the mounting board is equal to the desired finished width of the top treatment. Cut the board at least 1" (2.5 cm) wider than the window frame.

The length of the jabots should be in proportion to the overall width and look of the window. As a general rule, the jabots should end slightly above or below the middle of the window.

Select a fabric that has a nondirectional print so the lengthwise grain of the fabric can be run horizontally across the width of the window. This allows the swag to be constructed without piecing.

CUTTING DIRECTIONS

Use the full width of the fabric. Determine the cut length of the panel by measuring the desired finished length of each jabot and the length of the mounting board; add 1" (2.5 cm) for seam allowances. Cut the fabric and lining to this length.

For each tab, cut one fabric strip with a width of 6" (15 cm) and a length of about 28" (71 cm).

HOW TO MAKE A TAILORED SWAG

MATERIALS

- Decorator fabric.
- Lining, in same width as outer fabric.
- Mounting board.
- Staple gun and staples.
- Angle irons and pan-head screws or molly bolts.

1 Trim selvages from the outer fabric. For jabots with tapered lower edges, pin-mark 12" to 18" (30.5 to 46 cm) from corners at lower edge of fabric. Draw diagonal lines from pin marks to corners at upper edge. Cut on marked lines. Cut lining to same size, using outer fabric as a guide for cutting tapered edges.

2 Pin outer fabric to the lining, right sides together. Stitch ½" (1.3 cm) seam around all sides, leaving 12" (30.5 cm) opening at center of upper edge for turning. Trim the corners diagonally. Press the seams open. Turn right side out. Press edges, folding in seam allowances at center opening.

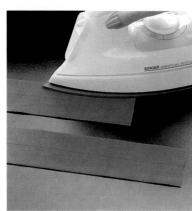

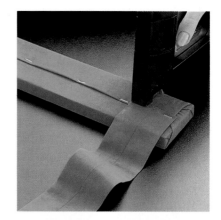

3 Fold tab strip in half, lengthwise; stitch ½" (1.3 cm) seam. Repeat for the remaining tab. Turn tabs right side out; press, with seam centered on the back side.

4 Cover mounting board as on page 16. Staple one tab, seam side up, to mounting board, with the raw edge centered and the pressed edge about ¼" (6 mm) from one end of the board. Repeat at opposite end.

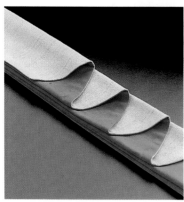

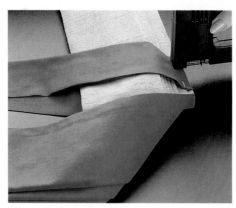

5 Place the fabric right side up. Fan-fold the entire width of the panel in about 4" (10 cm) folds, beginning at side opposite the longest edge.

6 Center folded panel on the mounting board, aligning longest edge to back edge of board; staple in place. Pull tab around to the front and adjust to desired position; turn under the raw edge of the tab and staple to board. Repeat for the remaining tab.

7 Mount swag as on page 17, steps 1 to 5. Tug gently on lower edge of center swagged portion to achieve desired look. Adjust tabs and arrange folds in swag and jabots; separate outer fabric and lining, if desired, for a fuller swag.

MORE IDEAS FOR TAILORED SWAGS

Braid trim (above) is used in place of fabric tabs to hold the swag in place.

Grosgrain ribbon (left) is stitched to the lower edge of the swag and jabots for contrast.

Fabric bows (below) are stitched to the tabs for a romantic touch.

BUTTERFLY SWAGS

Butterfly swags have a simple styling that works well for many decorating schemes. This lined stationary window treatment can be made in any length, from valance length to full length. Its fanfolded fabric is held in place with decorative straps. The folds swag in the center and flare at the sides, creating the butterfly effect.

The swag, attached to a mounting board, may be used alone or over a shade or blinds. If there is no undertreatment, a 1 × 2 mounting board can be used. With an undertreatment, use a mounting board that will project out from the window frame enough so the valance will clear the undertreatment by 2" to 3" (5 to 7.5 cm). The length of the mounting board is equal to the desired finished width of the valance.

The mounting board is installed at the top of the window frame, or just outside it, using angle irons a little shorter than the width of the board. Whenever possible, screw the angle irons into wall studs, using pan-head screws. For a secure installation into drywall or plaster, use molly bolts.

Butterfly swag can be sewn as a long window treatment (above) for privacy or as a valance (opposite) to enjoy the view.

MATERIALS

- Decorator fabrics, for swag and straps.
- Lining fabric.
- Mounting board.
- Heavy-duty stapler; staples.
- Angle irons; pan-head screws or molly bolts.

CUTTING DIRECTIONS

The cut length of the swag is equal to the desired finished length at the straps plus 25" (63.5 cm); this allows for the pleats, seam allowance, and mounting. To determine the width of the fabric, add the desired width of the swag plus 1" (2.5 cm) for the two seam allowances at the sides plus twice the width, or projection, of the mounting board. Cut the fabric and lining to this length and width, piecing fabric widths together, if necessary.

For straps with a finished width of 1½" (3.8 cm), cut two straps, 4" (10 cm) wide, with the cut length of the straps equal to twice the desired finished length plus 4" (10 cm); this allows for the mounting and the length taken up across the bottom.

HOW TO SEW A BUTTERFLY SWAG

1 Seam fabric widths, if necessary. Place the outer fabric and lining right sides together; pin. Stitch ½" (1.3 cm) seam around sides and lower edge; leave upper edge unstitched.

2 Clip lower corners. Press the lining seam allowance toward lining. Turn swag right side out, and press.

3 Fold one strap piece in half lengthwise, right sides together; stitch ½" (1.3 cm) seam on the long edge. Press seam open with tip of iron, taking care not to crease the fabric. Turn strap right side out, centering seam on back; press. Repeat for the second strap.

4 Determine desired placement for straps, 6" to 10" (15 to 25.5 cm) from end, depending on width of swag. Pin one end of each strap, right side up, to upper edge of swag at desired placement.

5 Wrap straps under bottom of swag; pin remaining end of each strap in place on lining side of swag, matching raw edges of straps to upper edge of swag.

6 Stitch outer fabric and lining together along the upper edge of swag, securing straps in stitching. Finish raw edges, using zigzag or overlock stitch.

7 Mark lines on top of the mounting board, 1" (2.5 cm) from front and sides. Center swag on board, with upper edge of the swag along the marked line. Staple in place at 2" (5 cm) intervals; apply two staples at each strap.

8 Wrap side of swag around end of the mounting board; staple in place on top of board, along marked line, forming a squared corner. Repeat for remaining side.

9 Secure angle irons to the bottom of the mounting board, near ends and at 45" (115 cm) intervals, using pan-head screws. Secure the angle irons to the top of window frame or to wall, using pan-head screws or molly bolts.

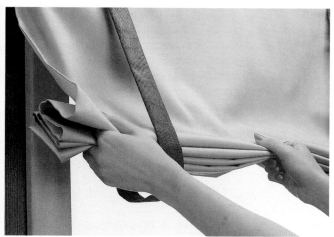

10 Fanfold the lower 24" (61 cm) of swag into five or six pleats, beginning by folding under the lower edge toward the lining.

11 Pull the pleats gently into swagged position at center. Adjust folds as desired near straps.

STAGECOACH VALANCES

Stagecoaches of the Old West were often fitted with simple shades that were rolled up from the bottom and tied in place. A variation of this shade makes a unique stationary valance.

The lower edge of the valance is rolled around a length of PVC plastic pipe, exposing the matching or contrasting lining, and tied with straps of fabric to give the illusion of an operating shade. If a patterned lining is used or if the lining is darker than the valance fabric, interline the treatment to prevent the lining from showing through to the front of the valance when light shines through the window.

The stagecoach valance is attached to a mounting board and can be installed inside or outside the window frame. When installed inside the frame, the ends of the PVC pipe are covered with matching fabric. For an outside mount, returns are added to the sides of the valance above the roll, and finials can be attached to the ends of the pipe.

Space the straps 24" to 36" (61 to 91.5 cm) apart, with the outer straps equal distances from the sides of the valance. For a valance that is wider than the fabric width, railroad the fabric (page 21) to eliminate the need for seams. If railroading is not possible, try to plan the placement of the seams to fall under the straps.

MATERIALS

- Decorator fabric, for valance and covered mounting board.
- Matching or contrasting fabric, for lining.
- Contrasting fabric, for straps.
- Drapery lining, for interlining, if necessary.
- 1¼" (3.2 cm) PVC pipe, cut to finished width of valance.
- Finials designed to fit 1⅜" (3.5 cm) wood pole and industrial-strength adhesive, for outside-mounted valance, optional.
- 1 × 2 mounting board for inside mount, length as determined on page 16.

- Mounting board for outside mount, length and width determined as on page 16.
- Angle irons with flat-head screws, for installing an outside-mounted valance, with length of angle irons more than one-half the projection of the board.
- 8 × 2½" (6.5 cm) flat-head screws, for installing an outside-mounted valance into wall studs; or molly bolts or toggle anchors, for installing outside-mounted valance into drywall or plaster.
- 8 × 1½" (3.8 cm) round-head screws, for installing an inside-mounted valance.
- Masking tape; staple gun and staples.
- Drill and ⅛" drill bit.

Stagecoach valance
*(above) is mounted
outside the window
frame. Decorative
finials are attached
to the ends of the PVC
pipe that supports the
fabric roll at the lower
edge of the valance.*

***Inside-mounted
stagecoach valance***
*(right) is mounted
flush with the front of
the window frame and
the ends of the pipe are
capped with fabric.*

Determine the finished length and width of the valance. For an inside-mounted valance, the width is ¼" (6 mm) less than the inside measurement of the window frame. For an outside-mounted valance, the finished width must be at least 1½" (3.8 cm) wider than the outside measurement of the frame, to allow the necessary space to mount the angle irons at the sides of the frame.

Cut the fabric for the valance with the length equal to the desired finished length of the valance plus 1½" (3.8 cm) for mounting plus 12" (30.5 cm) to roll onto the PVC pipe at the lower edge plus ½" (1.3 cm) seam allowance. For an inside-mounted valance, the cut width of the fabric is equal to the finished width of the valance plus 1" (2.5 cm) for seam allowances. For an

outside-mounted valance, the cut width of the fabric is equal to the finished width of the valance plus twice the projection of the mounting board plus ½" (1.3 cm) for seam allowances.

Cut the lining fabric to the same length and width as the valance fabric. Also cut the interlining, if desired, to the same length and width as the valance fabric.

For each strap, cut two fabric strips the entire width of the fabric, with the width of each strip equal to twice the desired finished width of the strap plus ½" (1.3 cm) for seam allowances.

Cut the fabric to cover the mounting board (page 16).

HOW TO SEW AN INSIDE-MOUNTED STAGECOACH VALANCE

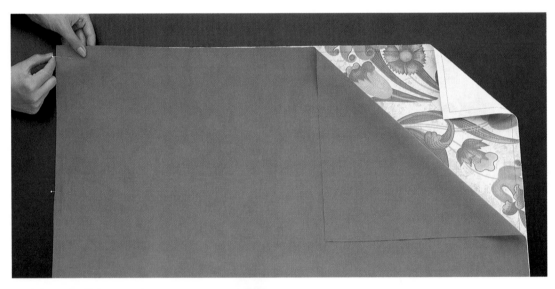

1 Seam fabric widths together, if necessary. Pin the interlining, if desired, to wrong side of the valance fabric; stitch to the valance fabric ⅜" (1 cm) from all edges. Pin valance fabric and lining fabric right sides together, matching the raw edges.

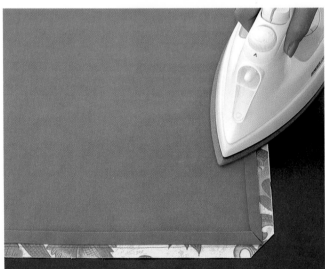

2 Stitch ½" (1.3 cm) seam around sides and lower edge. Trim seam allowances at lower corners diagonally. Press the lining seam allowance toward lining.

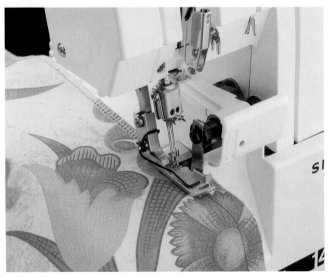

3 Turn valance right side out; press seamed edges. Finish upper edge of valance, using overlock or zigzag stitch.

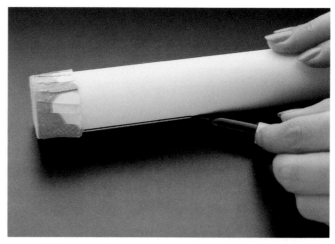

4 Cut two 3" (7.5 cm) circles of decorator fabric. On wrong side, trace circumference of pipe at center of each circle. Clip at ½" (1.3 cm) intervals from the outer edge to the inner marked circle. Glue to ends of PVC pipe, using craft glue.

5 Hold the pipe firmly in place on a table; place a marker flat on the table and slide it down the length of the pipe, to mark line down center of pipe.

6 Center the pipe on right side of valance at lower edge; tape in place, aligning the lower edge of valance to the marked line on pipe, using masking tape.

7 Roll up the valance to desired finished length. Anchor pipe in place with pins.

8 Fold fabric strips for straps in half lengthwise, right sides together. Stitch long edge and one short end, using ¼" (6 mm) seam allowance. Trim across corners diagonally, turn strap right side out, and press. Two straps are used at each placement.

9 Mark desired placement of straps at upper edge of the valance. Cover the mounting board (page 16); staple valance to the board, lapping upper edge of valance 1½" (3.8 cm) onto the top of board. Do not place staples at markings for straps.

(Continued)

10 Sandwich valance between two straps at placement marks; tack in place, using pushpins. Tie finished ends; adjust length of straps from upper edge, for desired effect, making sure all straps are the same length. Staple straps to board. Trim excess straps at top.

11 Mount the valance (page 17). Hand-tack rolled fabric to the front straps, catching only the back layer of fabric on straps. Remove pins that anchor valance to pipe.

HOW TO SEW AN OUTSIDE-MOUNTED STAGECOACH VALANCE

1 Seam the fabric widths together, if necessary. Fold the fabric in half lengthwise, right sides together. At raw edge opposite the fold, mark a distance 12½" (31.8 cm) up from lower edge.

2 Draw a line in from the side at mark, parallel to lower edge, with the length equal to the depth of return. Draw a connecting line, parallel to side, down to lower edge; cut out the section through both layers. The width at the lower edge should now be the finished width of valance plus 1" (2.5 cm).

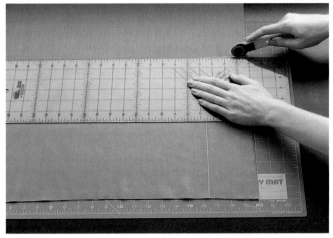

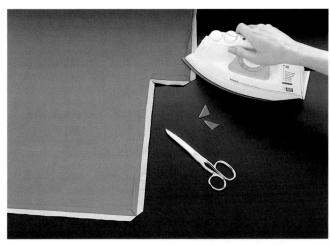

3 Repeat step 2 for lining, and for interlining, if used. Pin the interlining, if used, to wrong side of valance fabric; stitch ⅜" (1 cm) from all sides.

4 Pin valance fabric and lining fabric right sides together, matching raw edges. Stitch ½" (1.3 cm) seam around sides and lower edge. Clip and trim corners. Press lining seam allowances toward lining.

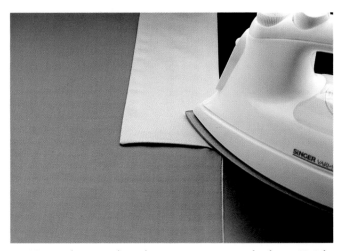

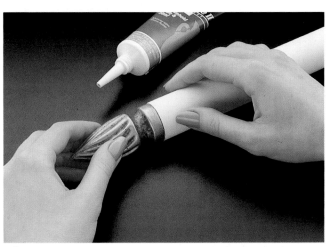

5 Turn valance right side out; press seamed edges. Finish upper edge of valance, using overlock or zigzag stitch. Press returns lightly.

6 Cover ends of the pipe with fabric, if desired, as on page 163, step 4. Or, for pipe with finials, sand ends of pipe smooth; glue finials to ends of pipe, using industrial-strength adhesive. Follow steps 5 to 8 on page 163.

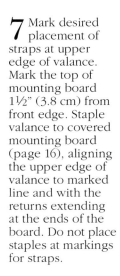

7 Mark desired placement of straps at upper edge of valance. Mark the top of mounting board 1½" (3.8 cm) from front edge. Staple valance to covered mounting board (page 16), aligning the upper edge of valance to marked line and with the returns extending at the ends of the board. Do not place staples at markings for straps.

8 Miter corners of returns; staple in place. Finish the valance as in steps 10 and 11, opposite.

BUTTONED VALANCES

Box-pleated valances give window treatments the look of tailored simplicity. With the lower corners of the pleats buttoned back, the contrasting fabric of the pleat inserts is revealed.

These valances are self-lined, eliminating the need for a lower hem. If the valance or the insert fabric is patterned and either lightweight or light in color, the valance should be interlined with lining fabric. Otherwise, the pattern of the self-lining would show through to the right side of the valance, especially with sunlight shining on the treatment.

Pleats are positioned at the outer front corners of the valance. If the projection of the mounting board is less than 5" (12.5 cm), the pleats are not buttoned back on the return sides of the corners. The number of remaining pleats and the spaces between them varies, depending on the size of the window, the desired valance length, and other design considerations. In some cases, it may be desirable to align pleats with existing divisions in the window space created by moldings or mullions, as shown in the diagram at right.

When planning the number of pleats and the spacing, also consider the fabric you are using. You may want to repeat a large motif in each space between the pleats, or perhaps a series of stripes. In general, a fabric with a solid color or a small all-over print can be divided into smaller spaces than a fabric with a large print. The wider the spaces and the larger the print, the more massive the valance will appear.

CALCULATING THE SPACES & PLEATS

Determine the finished width, length, and projection of the valance (page 18). It is helpful to diagram the window treatment. The spaces between the pleats should be at least 10" (25.5 cm) to allow enough room for them to button back. For a valance with evenly spaced pleats, determine the width of the spaces. To do this, first divide the approximate desired space measurement into the width of the valance, rounding up or down to the nearest whole number; this is the number of spaces between the pleats. Divide this number into the valance width to determine the exact measurement of each space. Including the pleats at the outer front corners, there will be one more pleat in the valance than the number of spaces.

MAKING A DIAGRAM

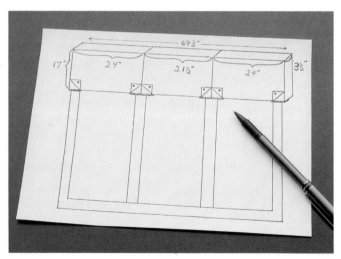

Diagram the window treatment, including any undertreatments. Label the finished length and width of the valance. Plan the placement of the buttoned pleats, with a pleat at each corner. Label the exact width of each space. Label the depth of the return.

MATERIALS

- Decorator fabric, for main valance fabric.

- Contrasting decorator fabric, for the pleat inserts.

- Lining fabric, for the interlining, if a lightweight or light-colored patterned fabric is used for valance or inserts.

- Covered buttons or decorative buttons in the desired size; one button is needed for each corner that will be folded back.

- Mounting board, cut to length as determined on page 16.

- Angle irons with flat-head screws; length of angle iron should be more than one-half the projection of board.

- 8 × 2½" (6.5 cm) flat-head screws for installing valance into wall studs; or molly bolts or toggle anchors for installing into drywall or plaster.

- Staple gun and staples.

Buttoned valances *have many design options. The look can be varied, as shown in the examples above, by changing the spacing between the pleats and the way the pleats are folded back.*

From the main valance fabric, cut the fabric for each space section with the cut width equal to the finished width of the space plus 1" (2.5 cm) for seam allowances; the cut length is equal to twice the finished length of the valance plus 3" (7.5 cm) for mounting.

From the main valance fabric, cut the fabric for each return section with the cut width equal to the projection of the mounting board plus 1" (2.5 cm); the cut length is equal to twice the finished length of the valance plus 3" (7.5 cm).

If the projection of the mounting board is more than 5" (12.5 cm), cut the contrasting fabric for all the pleat inserts 21" (53.5 cm) wide, with the cut length of the inserts equal to twice the finished length of the valance plus 3" (7.5 cm).

If the projection of the mounting board is less than 5" (12.5 cm), cut the contrasting fabric for the two corner pleat inserts with the cut width of each insert equal to twice the projection of the mounting board plus 11" (28 cm). For each remaining pleat insert, cut the contrasting fabric 21" (53.5 cm) wide. The cut length of all the pleat inserts is equal to twice the finished length of the valance plus 3" (7.5 cm).

If interlining is desired, the cut width of the lining fabric is equal to the total width of the valance after the valance seams are stitched. The cut length of the lining fabric is equal to the finished length of the valance plus 1½" (3.8 cm).

Cut the fabric to cover the mounting board (page 16).

HOW TO SEW A VALANCE WITH BUTTONED PLEATS

1 Pin the pleat insert for left end of the valance over the left return section, right sides together; stitch ½" (1.3 cm) seam.

2 Pin a space section to the pleat insert, right sides together; stitch ½" (1.3 cm) seam. Continue to join sections, alternating pleat inserts and space sections; end with the right pleat insert and the right return section. Press seams open.

3 Fold the end of the valance in half lengthwise, right sides together. Sew ½" (1.3 cm) seam on outer edge of returns; turn valance right side out, and press. Repeat for the opposite end of valance.

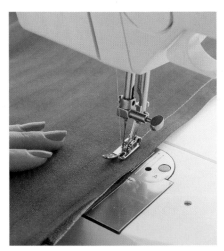

4 Press valance in half, matching raw edges and seams. Machine-baste layers together, ½" (1.3 cm) from raw edges at top of valance.

5 Mark center of each pleat insert along upper and lower edges. If return is less than 5" (12.5 cm), measure from inner seam of return a distance equal to twice the return; pin-mark.

6 Fold under pleats at all seamlines; press. Bring the pressed seams together to pin marks; pin pleats in place along upper and lower edges.

7 Press folded edges of all pleats, turning valance back and pressing only on the pleat, to avoid imprinting edges to right side of valance.

8 Stitch pleats in place across the valance, 1½" (3.8 cm) from upper edge. Finish the upper edge, using overlock or zigzag stitch.

9 Fold back lower corners of pleats at desired angle to expose pleat insert. Pin in place; press, if desired.

10 Determine button placement. Sew the buttons in place through all layers. For shank-style buttons, cut a small slit in the fabric, through corner layers only. Insert the shank through the slit; sew button through remaining layers.

11 Cover mounting board (page 16). Position the valance on the mounting board, using stitching line as guide to extend upper edge 1½" (3.8 cm) onto top of board; position end pleats at the front corners of board. Clip fabric at corner pleats close to stitching line. Staple the valance in place, beginning with returns; ease or stretch valance slightly to fit board, if necessary. Mount the valance (page 17).

HOW TO SEW AN INTERLINED VALANCE WITH BUTTONED PLEATS

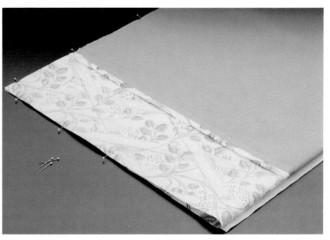

1 Follow steps 1 and 2, opposite; measure the width of seamed valance. For interlining, cut the lining fabric to this measurement, seaming widths together as necessary. Pin interlining to wrong side of valance, matching upper edges and ends.

2 Complete valance as in steps 3 to 11, opposite. The lower edge of interlining extends to the lower fold of valance.

TRIANGLE-POINT VALANCES

Contrasting band *of grosgrain ribbon outlines the lower and side edges of this triangle-point valance. Buttons and tassels accent the points.*

The dramatic lines of the triangle-point valance are softened by its gentle folds. It can be used alone or layered over the easy-to-sew curtain panels on page 61.

When a valance is hung from rings or decorative hooks, the look can vary, depending on the amount of fullness used. The valance above has two times fullness, the maximum amount recommended.

Opposite, the valance has about one and one-fourth times fullness.

To create a contrasting band of color along the lower and side edges of the valance, add a flat trim, such as grosgrain ribbon or braid. For more elegance, also add a button and tassel to each point of the valance.

MATERIALS

- Decorator fabric and lining, 48" or 54" (122 or 137 cm) wide; allow ⅝ yd. to ¾ yd. (0.6 to 0.7 m) for each fabric width needed.
- Grosgrain ribbon, decorative braid, or other tightly woven flat trim; allow 3 yd. to 4 yd. (2.75 to 3.7 m) for each fabric width needed.
- Decorator pole.
- Clip-on or sew-on drapery rings or decorative hooks.

CUTTING DIRECTIONS

Determine the desired finished length of the valance at the longest points; to determine the cut length of each fabric width, add 2½" (6.5 cm) to this length. Decide on the approximate fullness of the valance, no more than two times the finished width. Multiply the desired finished width of the valance times the desired fullness; divide this amount by the width of the fabric to determine the number of fabric widths required.

From the decorator fabric and the lining, cut the necessary number of fabric widths, making sure all crosswise cuts are at right angles to the selvage. Make a template for cutting the fabric as on pages 171 and 172, steps 1 to 4. Using the template, cut the points at the lower edges of the decorator fabric and lining as in steps 5 to 7.

Triangle-point valance from a decorator print fabric is used with easy-to-sew curtain panels (page 61).

HOW TO MAKE A TRIANGLE-POINT VALANCE

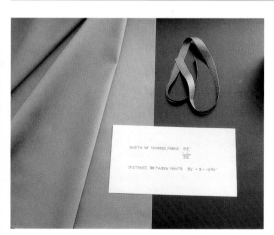

1 Trim selvages from fabric. Measure width of trimmed fabric; subtract 1" (2.5 cm), to allow for ½" (1.3 cm) seams on each side. To determine distance between lower points of valance, divide this measurement by 5; this allows for five lower points per fabric width.

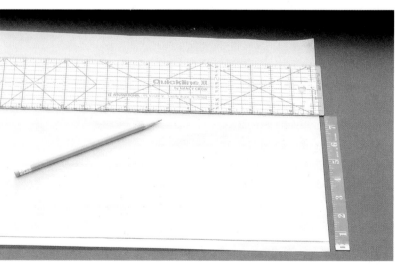

2 Cut a strip of paper, at least 10" (25.5 cm) long, with width of paper equal to the width of fabric minus seam allowances. Draw two lines across the strip, ½" (1.3 cm) and 7½" (19.3 cm) from lower edge.

(Continued)

171

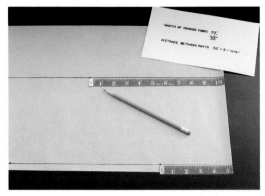

3 Mark upper angles of points on the upper line, spaced the distance apart determined on page 171, step 1. Mark the points of valance along the lower line the same distance apart, starting one-half the distance from edge.

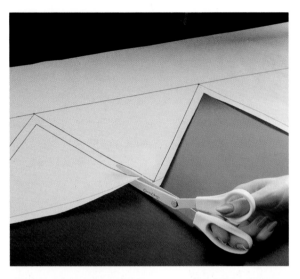

4 Draw lines between the upper and lower points as shown. Add ½" (1.3 cm) seam allowances at lower edge of the valance. Cut the template.

5 Seam the fabric widths. Place the decorator fabric on the lining, right sides together, matching raw edges. Place the template over the first width, with bottom of template along lower edge of fabric; place one end of template ½" (1.3 cm) from the raw edge of the fabric and the other end on the seamline. Mark cutting line for lower edge of valance on the fabric.

6 Reposition template on next fabric width, with both ends of template on seamlines; mark lower edge. Repeat for all widths.

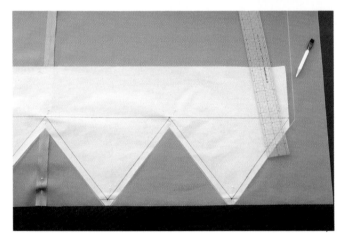

7 Cut partial width of fabric as shown, positioning the template with one of the upper points on seamline. Mark ½" (1.3 cm) seam allowance beyond the end of the template. Cut the valance and lining along marked lines; transfer the marked points from the template to the fabric. Pin layers together.

8 Sew ½" (1.3 cm) seam around sides and lower edge of valance, pivoting at points; leave the upper edge open. Trim seam allowances at lower points, and clip at upper points. Press lining seam allowance toward lining. Turn valance right side out; press along seamed edges. If the valance does not have trim, omit steps 9 to 11.

9 Preshrink grosgrain ribbon or braid trim by steam pressing it. Pin trim to one side of valance, with the end of the trim at the upper edge; match outer edges of trim and valance. Pivot trim at lower corner. Mark both edges for miter.

10 Continue to pin trim to lower edge and remaining side of valance; mark both edges for miters at the inner and outer points. Remove trim; stitch and press the miters.

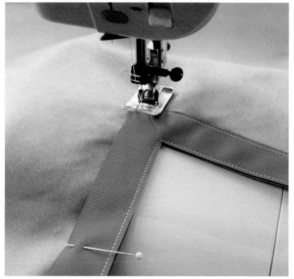

11 Repin trim to the valance. Edgestitch outer edge of trim around the sides and lower edge of valance, from upper edge on one side to the upper edge on opposite side. Edgestitch around the inner edge.

12 Press under 1" (2.5 cm) twice on upper edge, folding both layers as one; stitch close to fold.

13 Attach the rings or decorative hooks to the upper edge of the valance, positioning one at each end and one directly above each of the upper points.

14 Sew a button at each point and attach a tassel, if desired. If the loop on tassel is not large enough to go around the button, sew through loop when attaching button.

15 Hang the valance on decorator pole. Arrange valance for the desired drape between rings. Keep the rings from shifting, using floral adhesive clay or poster putty inside rings, along the top.

AWNING VALANCES

The simple lines of an awning valance make this window treatment suitable for many decorating styles, including contemporary, transitional, and country. Its classic style gives the look of a bistro to a traditional kitchen or porch. In a child's bedroom, it can be used to create a playful circus atmosphere.

The main body of the awning is constructed from one or more fabric widths with separate pieces for the rod pockets. Although the length of the awning may vary, a suitable length for most windows is 15" (38 cm).

The awning is supported by two curtain rods of equal length. If the awning is used between wall cabinets, a pressure rod is used for the upper rod. Otherwise a cafe rod is used for the upper rod; to provide a flush mount, the cafe rod is mounted with cup hooks instead of the usual brackets. For the lower rod, a canopy rod with an 8" (20.5 cm) projection is used, to hold the awning away from the window at the bottom.

CUTTING DIRECTIONS

Make the awning pattern as on page 176, steps 1 to 4; cut one awning piece from the outer fabric and one from the lining. For the upper rod pocket, cut one 3¼" (8.2 cm) strip from the outer fabric, with the length of the strip 2" (5 cm) longer than the rod width measurement from step 1. For the lower rod pocket, cut a 2" (5 cm) strip from the lining fabric; the strip is cut to the same width as the lower edge of the awning pattern.

MATERIALS

• Outer and lining fabrics.
• Cafe rod, 1" (2.5 cm) cup hooks, and plastic anchors sized for #4 screws, for upper rod if awning is not mounted between wall cabinets. Or pressure rod, for upper rod if awning is mounted between wall cabinets.

• Canopy rod with 8" (20.5 cm) projection, #4 screws, and plastic anchors sized for #4 screws, for lower rod.
• Drill.
• ⁵⁄₃₂" drill bit.

HOW TO MOUNT THE RODS FOR AN AWNING VALANCE

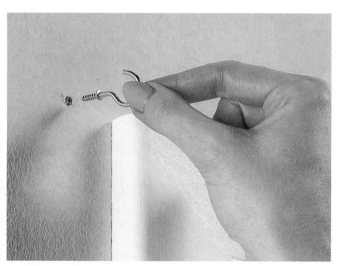

Cafe rod. Mark position for cup hooks about 1" (2.5 cm) outside and above window frame. Unless at wall stud, drill holes for plastic anchors, using ⁵⁄₃₂" drill bit. Tap plastic anchors into drilled holes; screw cup hooks into anchors. Repeat to install cup hooks at 36" (91.5 cm) intervals. Hang cafe rod on cup hooks. Lower rod is mounted after awning is sewn.

Pressure rod. Mount a pressure rod between cabinets at top of window, following manufacturer's directions. Lower rod is mounted after awning is sewn.

HOW TO MAKE THE PATTERN FOR AN AWNING VALANCE

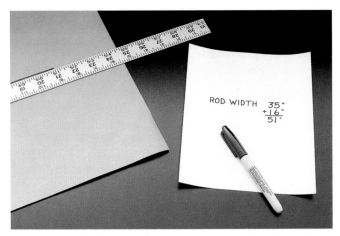

1 Measure the distance between outer cup hooks or the distance between the wall cabinets; this is rod width measurement. On tracing paper, draw a line for the lower edge of awning equal to rod width plus 16" (40.5 cm).

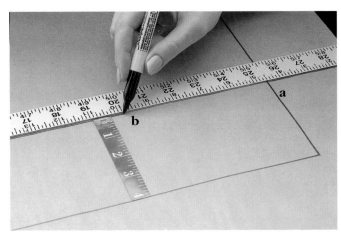

2 Draw perpendicular line **(a)** at each end of lower edge, equal to desired length of awning; 15" (38 cm) length works well for most windows. Mark a line **(b)** across width of pattern, 4" (10 cm) above lower edge; this is the drop length.

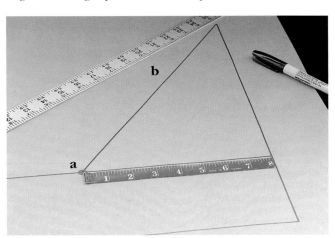

3 Mark a dot **(a)** on marked line for the drop length, 8" (20.5 cm) from each side; this marks the points of darts. Draw line **(b)** from marked dot diagonally to upper end of line for awning length; repeat for other side. Measure length of diagonal line.

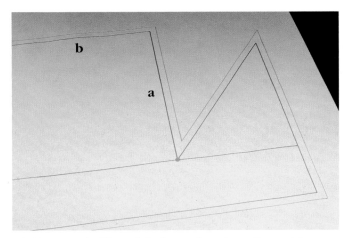

4 Draw vertical lines **(a)** of same length as diagonal lines, starting at marked dots. Draw horizontal line **(b)** across top of valance; this should measure same distance as rod width. Add ½" (1.3 cm) seam allowances on all sides.

5 Cut one awning piece from outer fabric and one from lining, piecing fabric widths as necessary. Transfer markings for dart points to wrong sides of the outer fabric and lining. Transfer line for drop length to the right side of lining.

HOW TO SEW AN AWNING VALANCE

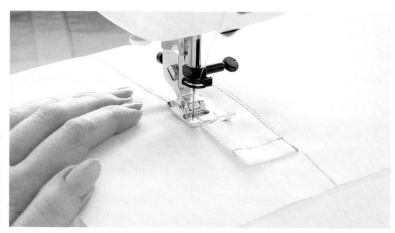

1 Press ¼" (6 mm) to wrong side on both long edges of lining strip for lower rod pocket. Turn under 1⅛" (2.8 cm) at ends; stitch. Pin strip to lining, with top of strip along the marked line for drop length and ends of strip ⅝" (1.5 cm) from the side edges. Stitch close to top and bottom of strip.

2 Stitch darts in outer fabric, ½" (1.3 cm) from raw edges, stitching to marked dots. Clip to point of each dart, and trim seam allowances near points; press darts open. Repeat for darts in the lining.

3 Press 1" (2.5 cm) to wrong side at each end of the fabric strip for rod pocket; topstitch in place. Fold fabric strip in half lengthwise, wrong sides together; baste raw edges together.

4 Pin rod pocket to upper edge of the awning piece from outer fabric, with the ends of rod pocket at dart seamlines and the raw edges aligned. Stitch ½" (1.3 cm) seam.

5 Pin outer fabric and lining right sides together; stitch around all edges, leaving 5" (12.5 cm) opening along side. Clip corners. Press lining seam allowances toward lining.

6 Turn the awning right side out; press seamline of rod pocket and edges of awning. Slipstitch opening closed. Fold and press awning along dart seamlines, right side out.

7 Insert rods into rod pockets. Hang awning from upper rod. Mark bracket positions for the lower rod, directly under cup hooks or ends of pressure rod. Install lower rod.

Soft cornices *may consist of a single padded panel (above) or, for more depth, of overlapping panels (right). Welting trims the lower edges and returns, but is optional at the top of the cornice.*

SOFT CORNICES

The soft cornice is a versatile top treatment with limitless possibilities. Lighter in weight and easier to construct than a traditional upholstered cornice, this softer version can be designed to work well in any decorating scheme.

A soft cornice can be constructed as a single panel of fabric with a shaped lower edge. Or, to add depth and texture to the treatment, it can be created with overlapping panels. Whichever style you select, use these basic construction steps as a springboard to creating truly unique soft cornices for your home.

Welting defines the lower and return edges of the soft cornice. For added definition, welting may also trim the upper edge; or, for a softer look, the welting may be omitted along the upper edge.

Decorator fabric is backed with fleece for a padded effect. To prevent the shadowing of any seams or overlapped panels, the cornice is lined with blackout lining.

The mounting board for the soft cornice is constructed with legs at the return ends to give the treatment added support. The finished width of the soft cornice must be at least 3" (7.5 cm) wider than the outside measurement of the window frame; this allows the necessary space at the side of the window frame for the legs and angle irons. Follow the basic guidelines on page 16 to determine the projection of the soft cornice and to mount the finished project.

As with any window treatment, it is important to diagram the soft cornice to scale. Hang a full-size paper pattern over the window before beginning the actual project, to check the measurements and proportion.

MATERIALS

- Decorator fabric for the soft cornice, hem facing, covered mounting board and legs, and dustcover.
- Contrasting decorator fabric and ½" (1.3 cm) cording, for welting.
- Flexible curve or curved ruler.
- Paper-backed fusible web.
- Polyester fleece.
- Blackout lining.
- Glue stick; heavy-duty stapler and staples.
- Mounting board and side legs; 8 × 2½" (6.5 cm) flat-head screws, for connecting legs to mounting board.
- Cardboard stripping.
- Self-adhesive hook and loop tape.
- Angle irons with flat-head screws; length of angle irons should be more than one-half the width of the mounting board.
- 8 × 2½" (6.5 cm) flat-head screws for installing soft cornice directly into wall studs; or molly bolts or toggle anchors for installing soft cornice into drywall or plaster.

DIAGRAMING THE SOFT CORNICE

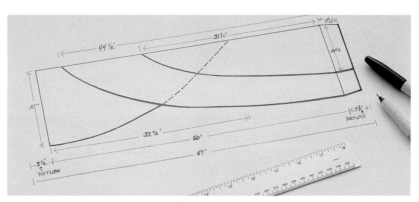

Diagram soft cornice to scale on graph paper. Indicate finished length at longest and shortest points, projection of mounting board, and finished width of cornice including returns. Indicate placement of welting with heavy lines; include ½" (1.3 cm) welting at lower edge and returns in finished length and width measurements. For cornice with overlapping panels, draw the shape of overlapped panels with dotted lines, and indicate the measurements of each panel.

For a single-panel soft cornice, cut the fabric with the length equal to the finished length at the longest point plus a 2" (5 cm) margin at top and bottom. The cut width of the fabric is equal to the finished width plus twice the projection of the mounting board plus a 2" (5 cm) margin on each side. If the cut width exceeds the fabric width, railroad the fabric (page 21) whenever possible, to avoid any seams. For fabric that cannot be railroaded, cut one fabric width for the center of the panel, and seam equal partial widths to each side, matching the pattern in the fabric.

For a soft cornice with overlapping panels, make the paper pattern pieces as on page 184, step 1. Cut the fabric, adding a 2" (5 cm) margin around each pattern piece.

Cut the polyester fleece, paper-backed fusible web, and blackout lining to the same size as the decorator fabric; the fusible web may be cut in several pieces, if necessary, butting the pieces together as they are applied.

For a single-panel soft cornice, cut one facing strip from the decorator fabric to the same width as the lining. To determine the cut length of the strip, subtract the shortest point of the cornice from the longest point; then add 3½" (9 cm). For a cornice with overlapping panels, cut facing strips for the panels on the return ends only. From the contrasting fabric, cut bias strips, 2½" (6.5 cm) wide, to cover the cording for the welting.

Cut the mounting board (page 16). Cut two side legs with the same projection as the mounting board, each 3" (7.5 cm) shorter than the finished length of the soft cornice at the return. Cut the fabric for the dustcover 1" (2.5 cm) wider and longer than the width and length of the mounting board.

HOW TO MAKE A SINGLE-PANEL SOFT CORNICE

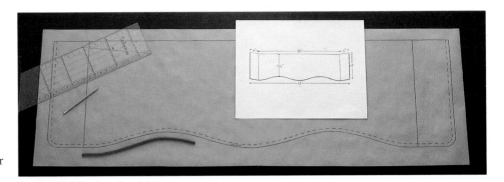

1 Draw full-size pattern of soft cornice, including returns, following scaled diagram (page 179); the ½" (1.3 cm) welting at lower edge and returns is included in the finished size. Use designing tool, such as flexible curve or curved ruler, to draw curved lines along lower edge of pattern. Round corners.

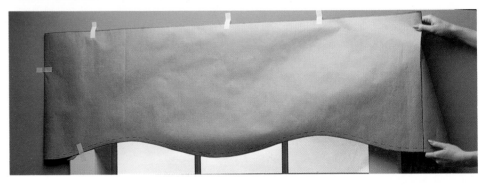

2 Cut out pattern; do not add seam allowances, because the ½" (1.3 cm) allowance for the welting compensates for seam allowances. Hang pattern in the desired location at top of the window; check for accurate measurements and proportion.

3 Place fabric facedown on pressing surface. Apply paper-backed fusible web to wrong side of fabric, following manufacturer's instructions; butt pieces of fusible web together as necessary.

4 Remove the paper backing from fusible web. Place the polyester fleece over fusible web; fuse in place, pressing from fleece side. Turn over; press again from right side of fabric.

5 Place the pattern on right side of padded fabric, positioning pattern as desired for design of fabric; pin in place within seam allowances. Cut out soft cornice along sides and lower edge; do not trim off the excess fabric at the top.

6 Press under ½" (1.3 cm) seam allowance along upper edge of facing strip. Lay facing strip over lining, right sides up, matching lower and side edges; glue-baste upper seam allowance of facing strip to lining.

7 Turn up the facing strip; stitch along pressed line. Turn the facing strip back down, realigning lower edges.

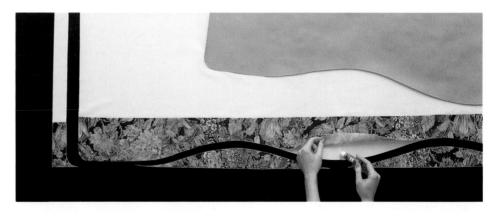

8 Place pattern facedown over the right side of lining piece, with the longest points of lower edge even with lower edge of the facing strip; pin within seam allowances. Cut out lining along the sides and lower edge; do not trim off excess fabric at the top. Glue-baste lower edge of facing strip to lining.

9 Make covered welting as on page 108, steps 1 to 3. Machine-baste welting to right side of padded fabric along sides and lower edge, matching raw edges and stitching a scant ½" (1.3 cm) from the edges. Clip and ease welting at corners and curves.

10 Pin welted fabric to lining within seam allowances, right sides together. Stitch ½" (1.3 cm) seam along the sides and lower edge, crowding the welting. Clip seam allowances on curves; trim corners. Turn soft cornice right side out; press.

(Continued)

11 Measure desired finished length from lower edge of the cornice; mark a line on the lining side. Mark a second line 1½" (3.8 cm) above the first line.

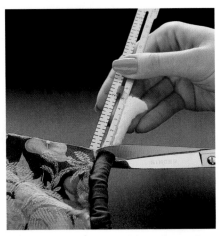

12 Cut along second line through all layers. Pull out cords at the ends of the welting; cut off 2" (5 cm) of cording.

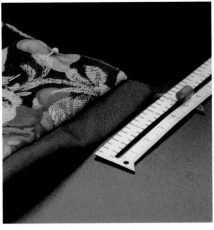

13 Pull seam to return the cords to original position. Finish upper edge by stitching through all layers, using zigzag or overlock stitch.

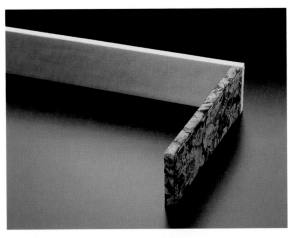

14 Cover mounting board and legs separately as on page 16, except attach fabric so fold is along the long edge of board as shown. Stand mounting board and leg on edge, with stapled sides facing outward; butt top of leg to underside of mounting board, with the outside edges even.

15 Predrill holes for two screws through mounting board into end of leg; insert screws. Repeat for other leg.

16 Support leg over edge of table; staple the hook side of hook and loop tape ½" (1.3 cm) from the back outer edge of leg, from the top of mounting board to the bottom of the leg. Repeat for opposite leg.

17 Cut two strips of loop tape to the same lengths as hook tape applied to legs. Affix to the lining at return edges of soft cornice, just inside the welting, with top of the tape at the marked line.

18 Place mounting board on lining side of the soft cornice, with front edge of the board facedown and the upper edge of the top board even with the marked line. Secure returns to legs with hook and loop tape.

19 Support mounting board on edge of work surface; staple the upper edge of soft cornice to the top of mounting board, clipping and overlapping fabric at corners. For soft cornice without welting at the upper edge, omit steps 20 and 21.

20 Trim ½" (1.3 cm) of cording out of end of welting; tuck fabric into end, encasing cord. Staple welting to top of mounting board, along the outer edge, beginning at back of board; allow welting to overhang cornice slightly. Staple to within 3" (7.5 cm) of opposite end.

21 Cut welting ½" (1.3 cm) beyond back edge of board. Trim ½" (1.3 cm) of cording out of end of welting; tuck fabric into end, encasing cord. Finish stapling welting to board.

22 Place dustcover facedown on cornice, with 1" (2.5 cm) extending over front edge onto top of mounting board and equal amounts extending at sides. Place cardboard stripping over dustcover, with edge of stripping along front edge of mounting board; if welting has been applied to upper edge, lay stripping even with seam of welt. Staple in place.

23 Fold back dustcover over cardboard stripping; fold under excess fabric on ends and along the back of the mounting board. Staple in place.

24 Mount soft cornice as on page 17, placing outer angle irons just inside legs of mounting board.

HOW TO MAKE A SOFT CORNICE WITH OVERLAPPING PANELS

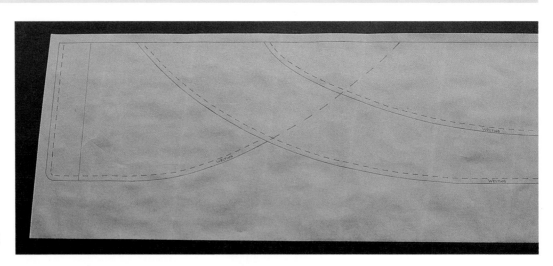

1 Draw a full-size pattern of the soft cornice, including the returns, following the scaled diagram (page 179). Draw separate patterns for each overlapping panel; include ½" (1.3 cm) welting in the finished size of each panel.

2 Tape pattern together as it is to be constructed, using removable tape. Hang in desired location at top of the window; check for accurate measurements and proportion.

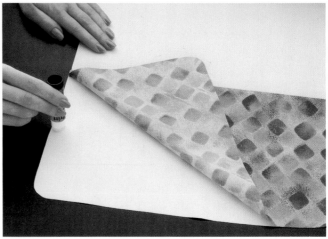

3 Separate the pattern pieces. For each panel of soft cornice, follow steps 3 to 5 on pages 180 and 181; for panels on return ends, apply facing strips as in steps 6 and 7. Continue as in steps 8 to 17 for all panels.

4 Arrange the panels on the mounting board in desired placement, tacking them in place temporarily, using pushpins. Secure return sides to legs of mounting board with hook and loop tape. Staple panels to mounting board.

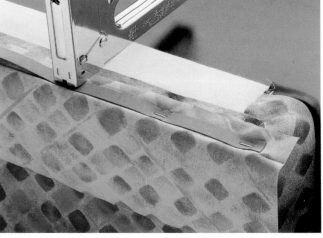

5 Follow steps 20 and 21 on page 183 if welting is desired along the upper edge. For a cornice with or without welting, complete the cornice as in steps 22 to 24.

MORE IDEAS
FOR SOFT
CORNICES

Triangle-point soft cornice
*(right) has overlapping panels
and is trimmed with welting. For
easier application of the welting,
the points are slightly rounded.*

**Soft cornice
with overlapping
panels** *(above)
is made using a
different fabric for
each panel.*

**Single-panel soft
cornice** *(left) is
shaped at the lower
edge to follow the
motifs in the fabric.*

VENT HOSE CORNICES

Create a playful, unique cornice using ordinary vent hose, available at hardware stores. Simply cover hose sections with fabric, and insert curtain rods into the hoses for a quick and easy, yet certainly eye-catching, top treatment.

For the cornice, use curtain rods with 5" (12.5 cm) projections. If the cornice is mounted over another window treatment, use valance rods with 7" (18 cm) projections. This allows for sufficient clearance between the undertreatment and the cornice; the vent hose itself takes up 1½" (3.8 cm) of the clearance.

For clearance at the sides of an undertreatment, mount the curtain rods for the cornice 2" (5 cm) beyond the rod for the undertreatment. If the cornice is used alone, mount the rods 2" (5 cm) beyond the window frame. Stack the rod brackets so the distance between the top screw holes is 3½" (9 cm).

MATERIALS

- Decorator fabric.
- 3" (7.5 cm) flexible aluminum vent hose.
- Three curtain rods with 5" (12.5 cm) projection.
- Heavy-duty hand needle and thread.
- Masking tape or white tape.

CUTTING DIRECTIONS

Stretch the vent hose to its full length. Cut it to the length of the curtain rod, including returns; allow slack for going around the returns and for a loosely scrunched look. Cut a strip of fabric 12" (30.5 cm) wide and two to three times the length of the rod; fabric strip may be pieced, if necessary. Repeat for each section.

HOW TO MAKE A CORNICE FROM VENT HOSE

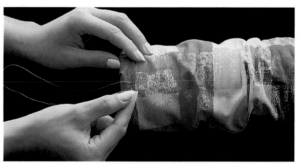

2 Fold ends of fabric tube to inside of the vent hose; hand-stitch in place. Insert curtain rod into the covered hose; bend hose ends at right angles to cover rod returns.

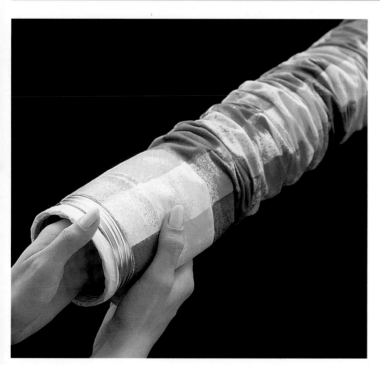

1 Seam the fabric strips together as necessary. Fold strip in half lengthwise, right sides together; stitch ¼" (6 mm) seam. Turn right side out, and press, avoiding any creases. Wrap tape around ends of vent hose. Slide fabric tube onto vent hose, leaving 1" (2.5 cm) of fabric extending beyond ends of hose; adjust fullness.

3 Repeat steps 1 and 2 for additional pieces. Install brackets (page 14), and mount rods, beginning with the bottom rod and working upward.

WALLCOVERING CORNICES

Use wallcovering borders to create sleek, tailored cornices. These cornices are especially attractive when used with simple undertreatments, such as shades, blinds, and sheer curtain panels. For a finished look, paint the edges of the cornice to match or coordinate with the edge of the wallcovering border.

Determine the inside measurements for the cornice only after any undertreatment is in place. The cornice should clear the undertreatment by 2" to 3" (5 to 7.5 cm), and it should extend at least 2" (5 cm) beyond the end brackets for the rod on each side. Choose a wallcovering border that is wide enough for the completed cornice to cover any drapery heading and hardware.

MATERIALS

- ½" (3.8 cm) finish plywood with smooth finish on at least one side.
- Wallcovering border; border adhesive; sponge applicator.
- Wood glue; wood filler; medium-grit sandpaper.
- 16 × 1½" (3.8 cm) brads; nail set.
- Primer suitable for paint and wallcovering.
- Paint to coordinate with or match the edge of the wallcovering border.
- Angle irons; pan-head screws or molly bolts.

CUTTING DIRECTIONS

Measure and cut the plywood for the top piece of the cornice to correspond to the inside measurements of the cornice, as necessary for the clearance of the undertreatment. Cut the cornice front piece to the expanded width of the wallcovering border (below). The cut width of the cornice front is equal to the width of the cornice top plus two times the thickness of the plywood. Cut the cornice side pieces equal to the expanded width of the wallcovering border by the depth of the cornice top.

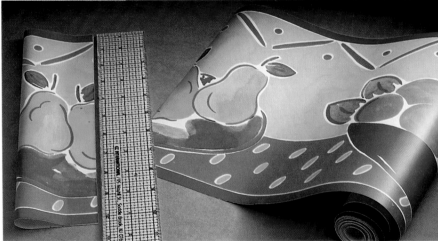

Determine the expanded width of the wallcovering border by applying border adhesive to a 6" (15 cm) length of border. Fold the border in half; allow to set about 5 minutes, then remeasure the width. This is the actual height to cut the cornice front and side pieces.

1 Glue and nail each side piece to the top piece, aligning upper edges; secure with nails. Glue and nail the front piece, aligning it to the top and side pieces.

2 Countersink nails. Fill nail holes with wood filler; fill front, sides, and lower edges of plywood as necessary. Sand front and side surfaces and edges smooth.

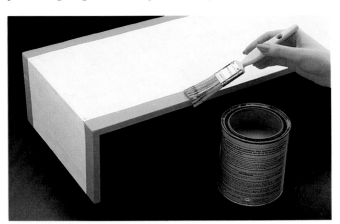

3 Apply primer; allow to dry. Paint lower edges and top of the cornice, extending paint slightly over edges to front and sides; paint inside of cornice.

4 Cut wallcovering border equal to distance around the sides and front of the cornice plus 4" (10 cm). Prepare wallcovering as for unpasted wallcovering (page 9), using border adhesive. Center wallcovering on cornice, wrapping wallcovering around the back edge of cornice just to the inside edge of plywood; trim excess paper.

5 Secure angle irons on inside of cornice top, near ends and at 45" (115 cm) intervals or less. Hold cornice at desired placement, making sure it is level; mark the screw holes on wall or window frame. Remove angle irons from cornice. Secure angle irons to wall, using pan-head screws drilled into wall studs, or use molly bolts. Reattach the cornice to installed angle irons.

MORE IDEAS FOR CORNICES

Border edging strip, *cut from a companion wallcovering border, trims the upper and lower edges of a shaped cornice.*

Stacked borders *add height to the cornice above.*

Scalloped border *at right is used to create a cornice with a shaped lower edge. The scallops are cut, using a jigsaw with a fine-toothed scroll-cut blade.*

*Alternative
Window
Treatments*

HANGING
PLANT SHELVES

Plants have a delightful way of adding charm and hospitality to a room, no matter what the decorating scheme may be. Placed on a hanging plant shelf, the plants receive the necessary light and serve as an attractive window treatment. Located near the top of the window, a single hanging shelf with several hanging or climbing plants becomes a valance. A double or triple hanging shelf, hung to cover the entire window or just the lower half, acts as a curtain when filled with plants.

The shelves, made from 1 × 6 stock lumber, are braced with parting stop at each end and suspended with rope from a wooden pole. When the pole is mounted at the top of a wide window, an additional brace and rope can be added to the center, along with a center support bracket for the pole.

The ropes are knotted just below the pole and under each brace to keep the shelf hanging level. If desired, holes can be cut into the shelf to hold pots that have slanted sides and collars, such as standard clay pots. Vary the number of the shelves and the space between them, depending on the size of the window, the height of the plants, and the desired placement of the plant shelves.

Holes cut into this hanging plant shelf hold potted plants of various colors, sizes, and shapes.

SELECTING PLANTS

Select plants for the hanging shelf according to the light requirements of the plants. Also consider other habits and features of the plants, such as the plant colors, their direction of growth, the size they will become, and their tolerance. Place plants of different sizes, shapes, and colors next to each other for contrast, or place several similar plants together for a more uniform look.

MATERIALS

- 1 × 6 boards, preferably of grade #2 or better.
- Parting stop.
- 180-grit or 220-grit sandpaper.
- Drill and 5/16" drill bit; 3/32" combination drill and countersink bit.
- 6 × 1" (2.5 cm) flat-head sheet-metal screws.
- 3/16" (4.5 mm) nylon or polyester rope.
- Wood pole, 1 3/8" (3.5 cm) in diameter, and finials.
- Pole brackets with 4" to 6" (10 to 15 cm) projection; center support bracket for pole measuring 36" (91.5 cm) or more, mounted at the top of a window.
- Latex paint, or wood stain and clear acrylic finish; sponge applicator.

CUTTING DIRECTIONS

Cut a 1 × 6 board for each shelf, with the length of the board equal to the outside measurement of the window frame. For the end braces under each shelf, cut two 7" (18 cm) lengths of parting stop. If the shelves are more than 36" (91.5 cm) wide, cut a third brace for the center of each shelf.

Mount the brackets for the wood pole as on page 197, step 10. Then, cut the wood pole 2" (5 cm) longer than the distance from the outer edge of one bracket to the outer edge of the other bracket. Cut a piece of rope for each end and for the center, if needed, with the length equal to twice the distance from the top of the pole to the bottom of the lowest shelf plus 6" (15 cm) for the upper knot plus 6" (15 cm) for each knot under each shelf plus an extra 6" to 10" (15 to 25.5 cm). Wrap tape around the cords before cutting, to prevent raveling.

HOW TO MAKE A HANGING PLANT SHELF

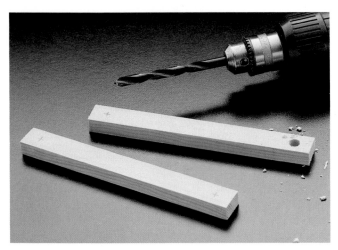

1 Mark placement of holes for rope on the wide side of braces, ½" (1.3 cm) from each end; drill holes, using 5⁄16" drill bit.

2 Sand all wood surfaces, using 180-grit or 220-grit sandpaper; round the corners of the shelves and braces slightly.

3 Mark lines on underside of shelf 2" (5 cm) from each end. On wide side of braces, mark placement for screws, 1½" (3.8 cm) from ends. Place braces, wide side up, on shelf, with outer edges along lines and ends extending equally on each side of shelf. Position a third brace, if needed, at center of board. Repeat for braces on any additional shelves.

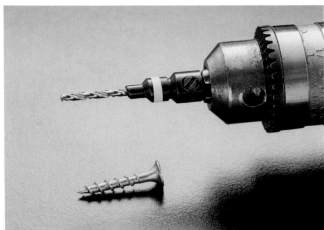

4 Adjust 3⁄32" combination drill and countersink bit as shown, so head of the drywall screw will be recessed below surface of wood when inserted into drilled hole; tighten set screw.

5 Predrill screw holes, holding the brace firmly in place as positioned in step 3; drill through brace and into underside of shelf, up to point on drill bit indicated by white line. Insert 6 × 1" (2.5 cm) drywall screw. Repeat for remaining braces.

6 Paint the shelves, if desired, or stain shelves and apply clear acrylic finish.

7 Fold the ropes in half. Tie each folded rope together in an overhand knot near the folded end, leaving a 2½" (6.5 cm) loop; tie all knots in the same direction so they look the same. Place ropes on work surface, aligning the ends and knots.

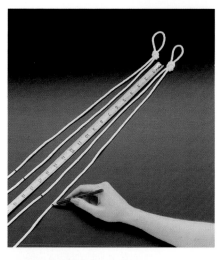

8 Measure from the overhand knots to the desired location for the first set of shelf support knots, allowing 1¼" (3.2 cm) for the thickness of the shelf and braces. Mark the ropes with pencil.

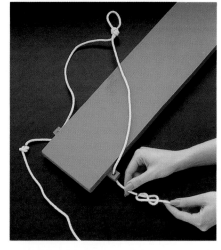

9 Thread the rope down through the holes in the braces of the shelf until the pencil marks are below the braces. As shown, tie a figure-eight knot at each location, just under mark.

10 Repeat steps 8 and 9 for any additional shelves, measuring from previous knots. Mount brackets for wood pole, either on the window frame or just outside the frame; use molly bolts or toggle anchors if not installing the brackets into window frame or wall studs. If a center support bracket is needed, mount it with one side of bracket at center.

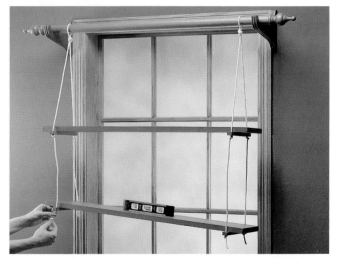

11 Slide the pole through loops in the rope, and attach finials to ends; mount the pole on brackets. Check to see that shelves are level and resting on knots; adjust the knots if necessary. Trim excess rope under the knots for the bottom shelf.

HOW TO MAKE A HANGING PLANT SHELF WITH INSERTED POTS

1 Mark placement for the ropes and drill holes as on page 196, step 1. Measure the circumference of flowerpot just under collar. Divide this measurement by 6.28 to determine radius. Draw a circle with this radius on paper, using a compass.

2 Cut out the circle; slide it over the bottom of the pot up to the collar; adjust the size of the hole, if necessary.

3 Determine the number of holes and spacing between them; the outer edge of first and last holes should be at least 3½" (9 cm) from the end of the shelf, and the minimum spacing between holes is 2" (5 cm). Mark circles for the holes on top of the shelf.

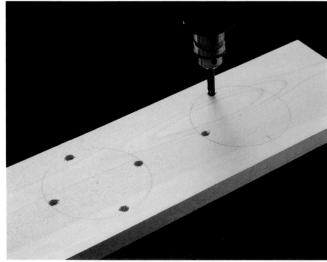

4 Drill four evenly spaced holes at inner edge of each circle, using large drill bit.

5 Insert jigsaw blade into drilled hole; cut on marked line up to next hole. Turn board, and continue sawing, turning board at each hole until entire circle is cut out. Repeat for remaining holes. Complete plant shelf as on pages 196 and 197, steps 2 to 11.

Potted ivy plants, hung at the sides of a window, climb the honeysuckle vine over the window frame. Secure the honeysuckle vines by wrapping them with wire and twisting the wire around screw eyes inserted into the window frame or wall. Loosely tie ivy stems to the honeysuckle vine, using string or plant ties; train new growth to climb by gently weaving it through the vine.

Spider plants (above), suspended from the ceiling at different heights, create an arched valance. The plant hangers with clear monofilament line are hung from ceiling hooks.

African violets (right) are hung at the sides of tieback curtains, using wall brackets designed for holding pots. Make the curtains as on pages 104 to 107, and make the shaped tiebacks as on pages 120 to 121.

Ivy window accents *add a romantic touch to a formal swag window treatment (top) or soften the look of a simple pleated shade (inset).*

IVY WINDOW ACCENTS

Embellish formal swags or soften window-shade treatments with silk ivy accents. Honeysuckle vines add interest and provide a base for securing the ivy. The vines are available in coiled bundles at floral shops. Although honeysuckle is rather messy to install, its pliable stems make it easy to work with. Add silk flowers to the arrangement, if desired. Stems with multiple blossoms are easier to arrange than individual flowers.

MATERIALS

- Honeysuckle vines.
- Silk ivy.
- Silk flowers, optional.
- Small screw eyes; medium-gauge wire; wire cutter.

HOW TO MAKE AN IVY WINDOW ACCENT

1 Secure screw eyes in upper edge of window frame, near ends, and spaced at 3 ft. to 4 ft. (0.95 to 1.27 m) intervals. Insert 18" (46 cm) length of wire through each screw eye.

2 Uncoil several of the honeysuckle vines. Starting at one end, wrap the wire around the vines. Twist wire to secure vines, concealing ends of wire.

3 Arrange ivy as desired, tucking the ivy stems into the honeysuckle vines to secure them.

4 Add flowers, if desired, inserting stems with multiple blossoms or individual flowers.

STAINED GLASS PANELS

A stained glass panel is a dramatic room accent. The beauty of the colors, the intricacy of the pattern, and the reflective quality of the glass are most evident when the panel hangs in a window. Stained glass panels may be custom-ordered. Used panels, removed from old buildings prior to demolition, are available at antique stores, thrift stores, and salvage yards. When selecting a stained glass panel, avoid those that are beginning to cave in, because they can easily collapse. If you find a stained glass panel that needs a replacement part, it can be repaired by a stained glass or leaded glass dealer.

Used stained glass panels will require cleaning and polishing. In addition to shining the stained glass, you may want to refinish or paint the wood frame. To display the panel, hangers may be secured to the frame.

HOW TO HANG A STAINED GLASS PANEL

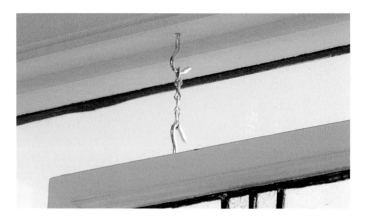

Secure hooks to the top of the stained glass panel frame and to the top of the window frame, predrilling the holes. Hang the panel from chains secured to the hooks. Use chains and hooks that are strong enough to support the weight of the panel, keeping in mind that the weight is distributed between the two sets of chains and hooks.

TIPS FOR REFURBISHING STAINED GLASS PANELS

Remove old paint from stained glass by applying mineral spirits to the area covered with paint, using a paintbrush; wait a moment, and scrape away paint with a razor blade. Or remove putty or glazing compound from the glass, using vinegar and a razor blade; do not use a heat gun, because it may crack the glass or melt the lead.

Clean dirty lead by rubbing 0000 steel wool over it, taking care not to scratch the glass; then wipe the lead with a dampened cloth.

Polish glass, using a commercial polish or a finishing compound; wipe the polish on, allow it to dry, and buff the surface. Or use furniture polish to shine the glass. Polish gives the glass a protective wax coating.

Clean glass, using a commercial-grade cleaner, if available; or use a standard glass cleaner.

FROSTED WINDOW DESIGNS

Here is a unique window treatment that is applied directly to the windowpane. Frosted glass spray paint provides a durable finish that cuts the glare of strong sunlight and provides privacy for windows in bathrooms or entrances. For a decorative effect, the paint is sprayed over a masking stencil of self-adhesive vinyl. The pieces of the stencil are then removed, revealing a clear design in the frosted glass. By reversing the stenciling process and masking the areas around the design, rather than the design itself, the spray paint can be used to resemble an etched design in the glass. Unlike true etched glass, frosted glass spray paint can be removed, if desired, using a razor blade or lacquer thinner. To clean the frosted glass without removing it, use a mild glass cleaner and wipe gently with a soft cloth.

MATERIALS

- Frosted glass spray paint.
- Self-adhesive vinyl, such as Con-Tact®.
- Mat knife.
- Graphite paper to transfer design, or precut stencil.
- Masking tape; paper.
- Glass cleaner; clean, soft, lint-free cloth.

Frosted glass with clear design (above) provides privacy, making it suitable for entrance windows.

Frosted design (left) adds detailing to a window, while allowing you to enjoy the scenery outside.

205

HOW TO APPLY A FROSTED GLASS FINISH
WITH A CLEAR DESIGN

1 Clean the window thoroughly, using glass cleaner and a soft, lint-free cloth. Cut self-adhesive vinyl 2" (5 cm) larger than design. Remove paper backing; affix vinyl to window in the desired location, pressing out any air bubbles. If more than one width of vinyl is needed, overlap the edges slightly.

2 Position design on window, with carbon or graphite paper under design; tape in place. Trace design onto vinyl (a). Or tape precut stencil to vinyl in desired position; trace design areas with pencil (b).

3 Cut around the design areas, using a mat knife, applying just enough pressure to cut through the vinyl. Overcut corners or curves into surrounding areas, if necessary, but do not cut into design areas.

4 Remove vinyl surrounding design areas, using tip of mat knife to lift edge of vinyl.

5 Press firmly on all areas of the design; rub away any traces of adhesive left on glass, using glass cleaner and a soft, lint-free cloth.

6 Mask off the woodwork around window and surrounding wall area, using masking tape and paper, to protect from overspray of the paint:

7 Check to be sure the glass surface is free of dust. Follow the manufacturer's instructions for applying paint. Spray paint onto the window in sweeping motion, holding can 10" to 12" (25.5 to 30.5 cm) away from glass, lightly respraying surface several times in one application. Allow to dry for 15 minutes. Repeat two or three times, for good coverage.

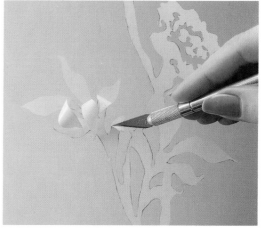

8 Remove vinyl in design areas, using tip of mat knife to lift edge of vinyl. Gently rub away any traces of adhesive left on the glass, using a soft cloth dipped in glass cleaner.

HOW TO APPLY A FROSTED DESIGN WITH SURROUNDING CLEAR GLASS

1 Follow steps 1 and 2, opposite. Cut around the design areas to be frosted, using a mat knife, applying just enough pressure to cut through the vinyl. At the corners, do not cut past point of the intersecting lines, onto the area surrounding design.

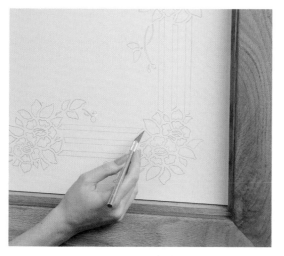

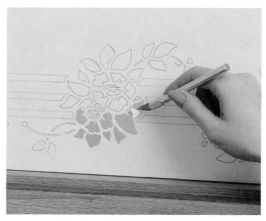

2 Remove vinyl in design areas to be frosted, using tip of mat knife to lift edge of vinyl.

3 Follow step 5, opposite. Mask off woodwork, walls, or any areas of the glass not protected by the stencil, using masking tape and paper.

4 Follow step 7, above, spraying over design area. Remove vinyl, masking tape, and paper. Gently rub away any traces of adhesive left on glass, using a soft, lint-free cloth dipped in glass cleaner.

SHOJI-STYLE
SCREENS

Traditional Japanese screens, called *shoji*, made by highly skilled craftsmen, are an intricate wooden lattice framework backed with rice paper. Muted light filters through the finely textured rice paper, filling the room with an aura of tranquility. A simplified version of the shoji can be easily made using basic tools and skills. These lightweight, stationary panels, with their clean-lined Oriental design, add sophisticated elegance to a room.

The shoji-style screen is made entirely from parting stop, which measures ½" × ¾" (1.3 × 2 cm). Cut from pine and other softwoods, parting stop is inexpensive and readily available at any lumber store. Although the wood in traditional Japanese shoji is left unfinished, this westernized version can be painted or stained, if desired. Traditional Japanese shoji are made with white rice paper, although colored or flecked papers that contain pulp and synthetic fibers can create interesting effects and may be more durable. The paper can be applied in one sheet or in multiple sheets, depending on the size of the paper you are using and the size of the shoji framework.

The screen may be mounted either inside the window frame or on the front of the frame. Careful measuring and cutting is important, especially if the screen will be installed inside the window frame. A frame depth of at least 2" (5 cm) is necessary for an inside mount, to allow the screen to be mounted flush with the front edge of the window frame, yet stand at least 1" (2.5 cm) away from the glass. The screen is made ¼" (6 mm) narrower and shorter than the inside of the window frame and is held in place by self-adhesive bumper pads secured to the outer edges of the screen to create friction between the window frame and the screen.

When the window frame is less than 2" (5 cm) deep, the screen is mounted on the front of the window frame, overlapping the inner edge of the window frame by ½" (1.3 cm). For windows with a sill, the screen overlaps the window frame on the sides and top and rests on the sill. Take accurate measurements of the window and draw a full-size pattern of the screen framework before cutting the wood.

Shoji-style framework *has an inner frame, consisting of two vertical stiles* **(a)** *and top and bottom rails* **(b)***, a slightly offset outer frame* **(c)***, and interior lattice strips* **(d)***.*

MATERIALS

- Parting stop; an estimate of the length needed can be made after drawing the pattern.
- Rice paper or other sturdy decorative paper.
- Double-stick transfer tape, or adhesive transfer gum (ATG) tape, available at art supply and framing supply stores.
- #6 × 1⅝" (4 cm) zinc-plated drywall screws, or deck screws.
- Wood filler; wood glue; sandpaper.
- Paint, or stain and clear acrylic finish, if desired.
- Self-adhesive bumper pads, ⅛" (3 mm) thick, for mounting the screen inside the window frame.
- Two shoulder hooks and two screw eyes, for mounting the screen on the front of the window frame.
- Mat knife.
- Spring clamps; drill; ⅛" combination drill and countersink bit.
- Small miter box and backsaw.

MAKING THE PATTERN FOR A SHOJI-STYLE SCREEN

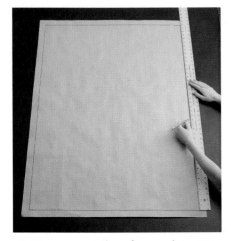

1 Measure window frame; determine outer measurements of screen as on page 209. Draw outline of screen on large sheet of paper; use accurate measurements and square corners.

2 Draw the outer frame of screen ½" (1.3 cm) wide; sides run full length of frame, with top and bottom sections abutting sides at inner edges.

3 Draw stiles and rails ½" (1.3 cm) wide, inside outer frame; stiles run the full length between top and bottom sections of outer frame, with rails abutting stiles at inner edges.

4 Draw inner lattice of screen as desired; draw all sections ½" (1.3 cm) wide, abutting the ends of lattice sections to inner edges of stiles, rails, or other lattice sections. Sections should abut each other at right angles. To allow for the insertion of screws, stagger placement of ends that abut opposite sides of the same section. It is helpful to plan the design of the lattice by sketching it on another piece of paper before drawing it on the pattern.

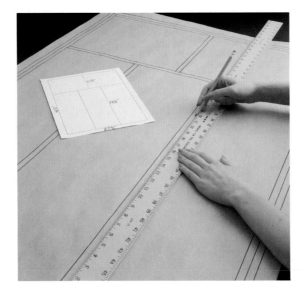

5 Tape the finished pattern to the window frame; check to see that the pattern is accurate.

HOW TO MAKE THE FRAMEWORK FOR A SHOJI-STYLE SCREEN

CUTTING DIRECTIONS

Measure the pattern for the length of each wood section, including the stiles, rails, lattice, and outer frame sections. Keeping the ½" (1.3 cm) side of the parting stop faceup, mark and cut the parting stop for each section, using a pencil; cut on the outside of the line, using a miter box and backsaw, leaving each section slightly longer than the desired finished length.

1 Check the lengths of outer frame sections by placing sections of parting stop over pattern. Sand the ends of sections until they fit the pattern exactly. Reposition on the pattern.

2 Repeat step 1 for stiles, rails, and all lattice sections until the entire framework is laid out on pattern.

3 Remove left stile from pattern, and place it faceup near the edge of a flat work surface. Abut bottom rail to stile, faceup, with lower edges even; clamp. Mark placement for screw on outside of stile, in line with the center of the rail.

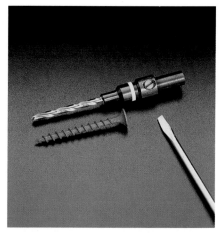

4 Adjust ⅛" combination drill and countersink bit as shown, so head of the drywall screw will be recessed below surface of wood when inserted into drilled hole; tighten set screw.

5 Predrill the screw hole, drilling through side of the stile and into center of the end of rail; countersink the hole up to point on bit indicated by white line. Insert drywall screw.

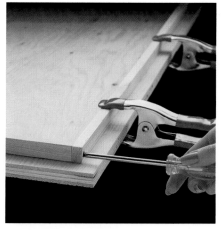

6 Repeat steps 3 and 5 for top rail. Attach right stile to the opposite end of rails, abutting ends of rails to side of stile; countersink holes, and insert screws.

7 Position the stiles and rails over the lattice pieces on pattern. Align all pieces for perfect fit. Make small pencil lines at every abutting location.

8 Join sections of lattice, working from center outward and aligning penciled markings. Keep lattice flat on work surface, and predrill holes in line with center of section being joined; insert screws.

9 Fit lattice inside the framework of stiles and rails. Join the stiles and rails to lattice, countersinking holes and inserting screws.

10 Apply wood glue to upper side of top rail and top ends of stiles. Place the framework faceup on flat surface; place straightedge of about ⅛" (3 mm) thickness next to top rail. Rest the top section of outer frame on straightedge to offset it slightly; glue to the top rail, aligning ends. Clamp in place.

(Continued)

11 Repeat step 10 for bottom section of outer frame. Then glue side sections of outer frame to stiles, using straightedge to offset them; align ends. Clamp in place until dry.

12 Cover exposed screw heads in lattice with wood filler, if desired. Allow to dry. Repeat if wood filler has shrunk. Sand filled areas until flush with wood surface.

13 Sand any rough areas of the screen lightly. If desired, paint the framework; or stain the framework and apply clear acrylic finish.

HOW TO ATTACH THE PAPER TO A SHOJI-STYLE SCREEN
USING A SINGLE SHEET

1 Cut rice paper 1" (2.5 cm) longer and wider than outer frame. Place screen framework facedown on flat surface; apply double-stick transfer tape to all styles, rails, and lattices.

2 Center piece of paper, right side down, and affix center of each side to frame.

3 Pull paper taut, and affix sides of paper to stiles and rails.

4 Affix the paper to all the lattice sections.

5 Fold back the excess paper at the edges of inner frame; crease. Trim, using mat knife.

HOW TO ATTACH THE PAPER TO A SHOJI-STYLE SCREEN USING MULTIPLE SHEETS

1 Divide original screen pattern into smaller areas if one sheet of paper is not large enough to cover the entire screen. Trace each area onto tracing paper, planning for paper pieces to overlap each other on the back of the lattice sections, hiding seams.

2 Cut each piece of paper, using traced patterns; add a 1" (2.5 cm) margin on each side.

3 Place screen framework facedown on flat surface. Apply double-stick transfer tape to outer edges of first area to be covered and to any lattice strips within the area.

4 Center corresponding piece of paper, right side down, and affix center of each side to frame.

5 Pull paper taut, and affix to edges. Fold back excess paper at edges; crease. Trim, using mat knife.

6 Apply paper to adjoining area, overlapping pieces on the back of any adjoining lattice strips. Continue to apply each piece consecutively, working from one end of screen to the other.

HOW TO MOUNT A SHOJI-STYLE SCREEN INSIDE THE WINDOW FRAME

1 Remove the protective cover from self-adhesive bumper pads, and secure to outside edge of outer frame, 2" (5 cm) from each corner. Secure additional pads at 18" to 24" (46 to 61 cm) intervals around outer frame.

2 Push the screen into place inside the window frame until front of screen is flush with front of the window frame. Check for snug fit. Stack additional pads, if necessary.

HOW TO MOUNT A SHOJI-STYLE SCREEN ON THE FRONT OF THE WINDOW FRAME

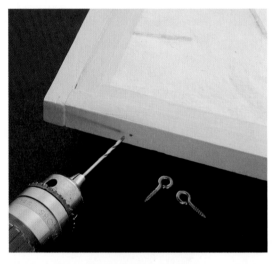

1 Mark placement for screw eyes on top of the outer frame, 2" (5 cm) from the corners. Predrill holes, using a drill bit slightly smaller than diameter of threaded portion of screw eye. Insert screw eyes.

2 Hold screen in place at window, overlapping window frame ½" (1.3 cm). Mark placement for shoulder hooks.

3 Predrill the holes for shoulder hooks, using a drill bit slightly smaller than diameter of threaded portion of hook. Insert hooks.

4 Hang the screen, hooking the screw eyes over the shoulder hooks.

MORE IDEAS FOR DESIGNING SHOJI-STYLE SCREENS

Multicolor screen *with a painted frame is mounted over a door window for privacy.*

Textured white papers *are used for this inside-mounted screen. The screen has been stained to match the window frame.*

CREATIVE ALTERNATIVES

Unique window treatments can be created from items intended for other purposes. Consider using beautiful table linens to dress your windows. A favorite collection of hats or fans can be turned into an eye-catching valance. Unexpected elements used as window treatments add charm and personality to your home.

Hanging shelf valance *(page 194), shown above, makes an ideal swing for teddy bears in a child's bedroom.*

Decorative papers
(above) layered over a
pole create a valance
with a contemporary
look. The papers are
secured to the rod with
double-stick tape.

Leather belts
buckled over a rolled
matchstick blind
create a masculine
stagecoach valance.
When mounting the
shade, drill the holes
and insert the screws
through the belts and
the mounting board.

(Continued)

CREATIVE
ALTERNATIVES
(CONTINUED)

Embroidered table runners (left) are draped over swag holders for a simple, yet striking, swag.

Straw hats (below), adorned with flowers and ribbons, are hung from a peg rail to create a seasonal window valance.

Sports pennants
(above) create a
fitting treatment
for a young sports
fan. The pennants
are secured to the
wood pole with
double-stick tape.

**Seining net and
creels** (right)
balance each other
in a rustic display.

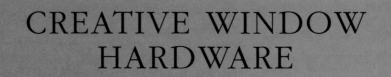

CREATIVE WINDOW HARDWARE

A wide variety of objects can be used for creative window hardware. Let your interests and your decorating style guide you. Consider yokes and metal spurs for Western or country decorating. If boating is your favorite pastime, use an old oar, perhaps with fishing tackle and a fish net. A golf club can become a curtain rod in an enthusiast's den.

Boat oar serves as a rustic curtain rod for a swagged window treatment.

Metal spurs (left) become tieback holders for a Western decorating style.

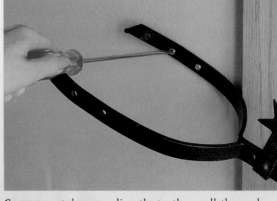

Screw metal spurs directly to the wall through the holes in the spurs.

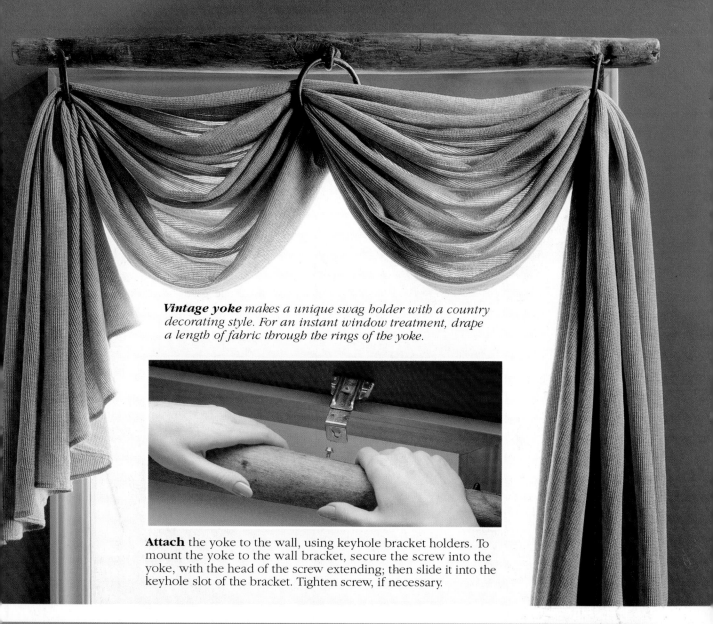

Vintage yoke makes a unique swag holder with a country decorating style. For an instant window treatment, drape a length of fabric through the rings of the yoke.

Attach the yoke to the wall, using keyhole bracket holders. To mount the yoke to the wall bracket, secure the screw into the yoke, with the head of the screw extending; then slide it into the keyhole slot of the bracket. Tighten screw, if necessary.

...lking cane, attached with keyhole bracket holders as shown above, makes a creative curtain rod, and a wool ...anket becomes the curtain. Thread the blanket onto the rod through slits cut along the top of the blanket.

INDEX